THE COLLECTED POETRY OF D. H. LAWRENCE

A Digireads.com Book
Digireads.com Publishing

The Collected Poetry of D. H. Lawrence
By D. H. Lawrence
ISBN 10: 1-4209-4750-8
ISBN 13: 978-1-4209-4750-2

Please visit *www.digireads.com*

CONTENTS

LOVE AND OTHER POEMS (1915)

AMORES (1916)

4

LOOK! WE HAVE COME THROUGH! (1917)

6

NEW POEMS (1918)

BAY . . A BOOK OF . . POEMS (1919)

TORTOISES (1921)

8

LOVE AND OTHER POEMS (1915)

WEDDING MORN

The morning breaks like a pomegranate
    In a shining crack of red,
Ah, when tomorrow the dawn comes late
    Whitening across the bed,
It will find me watching at the marriage gate
    And waiting while light is shed
On him who is sleeping satiate,
    With a sunk, abandoned head.

And when the dawn comes creeping in,
    Cautiously I shall raise
Myself to watch the morning win
    My first of days,
As it shows him sleeping a sleep he got
    Of me, as under my gaze,
He grows distinct, and I see his hot
    Face freed of the wavering blaze.

Then I shall know which image of God
    My man is made toward,
And I shall know my bitter rod
    Or my rich reward.
And I shall know the stamp and worth
    Of the coin I've accepted as mine,
Shall see an image of heaven or of earth
    On his minted metal shine.

Yea and I long to see him sleep
    In my power utterly,
I long to know what I have to keep,
    I long to see
My love, that spinning coin, laid still
    And plain at the side of me,
For me to count—for I know he will
    Greatly enrichen me.

And then he will be mine, he will lie
    In my power utterly,
Opening his value plain to my eye
    He will sleep of me.
He will lie negligent, resign
    His all to me, and I
Shall watch the dawn light up for me
    This sleeping wealth of mine.

And I shall watch the wan light shine
    On his sleep that is filled of me,
On his brow where the wisps of fond hair twine
    So truthfully,
On his lips where the light breaths come and go
    Naïve and winsomely,
On his limbs that I shall weep to know
    Lie under my mastery.

KISSES IN THE TRAIN

I saw the midlands
    Revolve through her hair;
The fields of autumn
    Stretching bare,
And sheep on the pasture
    Tossed back in a scare.

And still as ever
    The world went round,
My mouth on her pulsing
    Neck was found,
And my breast to her beating
    Breast was bound.

But my heart at the centre
    Of all, in a swound
Was still as a pivot,
    As all the ground
On its prowling orbit
    Shifted round.

And still in my nostrils
    The scent of her flesh,
And still my wet mouth
    Sought her afresh;
And still one pulse
    Through the world did thresh.

And the world all whirling
   Around in joy
Like the dance of a dervish
   Did destroy
My sense—and my reason
   Spun like a toy.

But firm at the centre
   My heart was found;
Her own to my perfect
   Heart-beat bound,
Like a magnet's keeper
   Closing the round.

CRUELTY AND LOVE

What large, dark hands are those at the window
Lifted, grasping the golden light
Which weaves its way through the creeper leaves
      To my heart's delight?

Ah, only the leaves! But in the west,
In the west I see a redness come
Over the evening's burning breast—
      —'Tis the wound of love goes home!

  The woodbine creeps abroad
  Calling low to her lover:
    The sun-lit flirt who all the day
    Has poised above her lips in play
    And stolen kisses, shallow and gay
    Of pollen, now has gone away
    —She woos the moth with her sweet, low word,
  And when above her his broad wings hover
  Then her bright breast she will uncover
  And yield her honey-drop to her lover.

Into the yellow, evening glow
Saunters a man from the farm below,
Leans, and looks in at the low-built shed
Where hangs the swallow's marriage bed.
  The bird lies warm against the wall.
  She glances quick her startled eyes
  Towards him, then she turns away
  Her small head, making warm display
  Of red upon the throat. His terrors sway
  Her out of the nest's warm, busy ball,

Whose plaintive cry is heard as she flies
In one blue stoop from out the sties
Into the evening's empty hall.

Oh, water-hen, beside the rushes
Hide your quaint, unfading blushes,
Still your quick tail, and lie as dead,
Till the distance folds over his ominous tread.

The rabbit presses back her ears,
Turns back her liquid, anguished eyes
And crouches low: then with wild spring
Spurts from the terror of *his* oncoming
To be choked back, the wire ring
Her frantic effort throttling:
    Piteous brown ball of quivering fears!

Ah soon in his large, hard hands she dies,
And swings all loose to the swing of his walk.
Yet calm and kindly are his eyes
And ready to open in brown surprise
Should I not answer to his talk
Or should he my tears surmise.

I hear his hand on the latch, and rise from my chair
Watching the door open: he flashes bare
His strong teeth in a smile, and flashes his eyes
In a smile like triumph upon me; then careless-wise
He flings the rabbit soft on the table board
And comes towards me: ah, the uplifted sword
Of his hand against my bosom, and oh, the broad
Blade of his hand that raises my face to applaud
His coming: he raises up my face to him
And caresses my mouth with his fingers, which still smell grim
Of the rabbit's fur! God, I am caught in a snare!
I know not what fine wire is round my throat,
I only know I let him finger there
My pulse of life, letting him nose like a stoat
Who sniffs with joy before he drinks the blood:
And down his mouth comes to my mouth, and down
His dark bright eyes descend like a fiery hood
Upon my mind: his mouth meets mine, and a flood
Of sweet fire sweeps across me, so I drown
Within him, die, and find death good.

CHERRY ROBBERS

Under the long, dark boughs, like jewels red
    In the hair of an Eastern girl
Shine strings of crimson cherries, as if had bled
    Blood-drops beneath each curl.

Under the glistening cherries, with folded wings
    Three dead birds lie:
Pale-breasted throstles and a blackbird, robberlings
    Stained with red dye.

Under the haystack a girl stands laughing at me,
    With cherries hung round her ears—
Offering me her scarlet fruit: I will see
    If she has any tears.

LILIES IN THE FIRE

I

Ah, you stack of white lilies, all white and gold,
A am adrift as a sunbeam, and without form
Or having, save I light on you to warm
Your pallor into radiance, flush your cold

White beauty into incandescence: you
Are not a stack of white lilies tonight, but a white
And clustered star transfigured by me tonight,
And lighting these ruddy leaves like a star dropped through

The slender bare arms of the branches, your tire-maidens
Who lift swart arms to fend me off; but I come
Like a wind of fire upon you, like to some
Stray whitebeam who on you his fire unladens.

And you are a glistening toadstool shining here
Among the crumpled beech-leaves phosphorescent,
My stack of white lilies burning incandescent
Of me, a soft white star among the leaves, my dear.

II

Is it with pain, my dear, that you shudder so?
Is it because I have hurt you with pain, my dear?

14

Did I shiver?—Nay, truly I did not know—
A dewdrop may-be splashed on my face down here.
Why even now you speak through close-shut teeth,
I have been too much for you—Ah, I remember!
   The ground is a little chilly underneath
   The leaves—and, dear, you consume me all to an ember.

You hold yourself all hard as if my kisses
Hurt as I gave them—you put me away—

   Ah never I put you away: yet each kiss hisses
   Hot as a drop of fire wastes me away.

III

I am ashamed, you wanted me not to-night—
Nay, it is always so, you sigh with me.
Your radiance dims when I draw too near, and my free
Fire enters your petals like death, you wilt dead white.

Ah, I do know, and I am deep ashamed;
You love me while I hover tenderly
Like clinging sunbeams kissing you: but see
When I close in fire upon you, and you are flamed

With the swiftest fire of my love, you are destroyed.
'Tis a degradation deep to me, that my best
Soul's whitest lightning which should bright attest
God stepping down to earth in one white stride,

Means only to you a clogged, numb burden of flesh
Heavy to bear, even heavy to uprear
Again from earth, like lilies wilted and sere
Flagged on the floor, that before stood up so fresh.

COLDNESS IN LOVE

And you remember, in the afternoon
The sea and the sky went grey, as if there had sunk
A flocculent dust on the floor of the world: the festoon
Of the sky sagged dusty as spider cloth,
And coldness clogged the sea, till it ceased to croon.

A dank, sickening scent came up from the grime
Of weed that blackened the shore, so that I recoiled
Feeling the raw cold dun me: and all the time
You leapt about on the slippery rocks, and threw
The words that rang with a brassy, shallow chime.

And all day long that raw and ancient cold
Deadened me through, till the grey downs darkened to sleep.
Then I longed for you with your mantle of love to fold
Me over, and drive from out of my body the deep
Cold that had sunk to my soul, and there kept hold.

But still to me all evening long you were cold,
And I was numb with a bitter, deathly ache;
Till old days drew me back into their fold,
And dim sheep crowded me warm with companionship,
And old ghosts clustered me close, and sleep was cajoled.

I slept till dawn at the window blew in like dust,
Like the linty, raw-cold dust disturbed from the floor
Of a disused room: a grey pale light like must
That settled upon my face and hands till it seemed
To flourish there, as pale mould blooms on a crust.

Then I rose in fear, needing you fearfully,
For I thought you were warm as a sudden jet of blood.
I thought I could plunge in your spurting hotness, and be
Clean of the cold and the must.—With my hand on the latch
I heard you in your sleep speak strangely to me.

And I dared not enter, feeling suddenly dismayed.
So I went and washed my deadened flesh in the sea
And came back tingling clean, but worn and frayed
With cold, like the shell of the moon: and strange it seems
That my love has dawned in rose again, like the love of a maid.

END OF ANOTHER HOME-HOLIDAY

When shall I see the half-moon sink again
Behind the black sycamore at the end of the garden?
When will the scent of the dim white phlox
Creep up the wall to me, and in at my open window?

Why is it, the long, slow stroke of the midnight bell
   (Will it never finish the twelve?)
Falls again and again on my heart with a heavy reproach?

The moon-mist is over the village, out of the mist speaks the bell,
And all the little roofs of the village bow low, pitiful, beseeching,
resigned.
    Oh, little home! what is it I have not done well?

Ah home, suddenly I love you
As I hear the sharp clean trot of a pony down the road,
Succeeding sharp little sounds dropping into silence
Clear upon the long-drawn hoarseness of a train across the valley.

The light has gone out, from under my mother's door.
    That she should love me so!–
    She, so lonely, greying now!
    And I leaving her,
    Bent on my pursuits!

    Love is the great Asker.
    The sun and the rain do not ask the secret
    Of the time when the grain struggles down in the dark.
    The moon walks her lonely way without anguish,
    Because no-one grieves over her departure.

II

    Forever, ever by my shoulder pitiful love will linger,
    Crouching as little houses crouch under the mist when I turn.

Forever, out of the mist, the church lifts up a reproachful finger
Pointing my eyes in wretched defiance where love hides her face to mourn.

    Oh! but the rain creeps down to wet the grain
    That struggles alone in the dark,
    And asking nothing, patiently steals back again!
    The moon sets forth o'nights
    To walk the lonely, dusky heights
    Serenely, with steps unswerving;
    Pursued by no sigh of bereavement,
    No tears of love unnerving
    Her constant tread
    While ever at my side,
    Frail and sad, with grey, bowed head,
    The beggar-woman, the yearning-eyed
    Inexorable love goes lagging.

The wild young heifer, glancing distraught,
With a strange new knocking of life at her side
Runs seeking a loneliness.

The little grain draws down the earth, to hide.
Nay, even the slumberous egg, as it labours under the shell
   Patiently to divide and self-divide,
Asks to be hidden, and wishes nothing to tell.

But when I draw the scanty cloak of silence over my eyes
Piteous love comes peering under the hood;
Touches the clasp with trembling fingers, and tries
To put her ear to the painful sob of my blood;
While her tears soak through to my breast,
   Where they burn and cauterize.

III

The moon lies back and reddens.
In the valley a corncrake calls
   Monotonously,
With a plaintive, unalterable voice, that deadens
   My confident activity;
With a hoarse, insistent request that falls
   Unweariedly, unweariedly,
   Asking something more of me,
     Yet more of me.

REMINDER

   Do you remember
How night after night swept level and low
Overhead, at home, and had not one star,
Nor one narrow gate for the moon to go
   Forth to her field of November.

   And you remember,
How towards the north a red blot on the sky
Burns like a blotch of anxiety
Over the forges, and small flames ply
   Like ghosts the shadow of the ember.

   Those were the days
When it was awful autumn to me,
When only there glowed on the dark of the sky
The red reflection of her agony,
   My beloved smelting down in the blaze

   Of death—my dearest
Love who had borne, and was now leaving me.
And I at the foot of her cross did suffer
   My own gethsemane.

So I came to you,
And twice, after great kisses, I saw
The rim of the moon divinely rise
And strive to detach herself from the raw
    Blackened edge of the skies.

Strive to escape;
With her whiteness revealing my sunken world
Tall and loftily shadowed. But the moon
Never magnolia-like unfurled
    Her white, her lamp-like shape.

For you told me no,
And bade me not to ask for the dour
Communion, offering—"a better thing."
So I lay on your breast for an obscure hour
    Feeling your fingers go

Like a rhythmic breeze
Over my hair, and tracing my brows,
Till I knew you not from a little wind:
—I wonder now if God allows
    Us only one moment of his keys.

If only then
You could have unlocked the moon on the night,
And I baptized myself in the light
Of your love; we both have entered then the white
    Pure passion, and never again.

I wonder if only
You had taken me then, how different
Life would have been: should I have spent
Myself in waste, and you have bent
    Your pride, through being lonely?

BEI HENNEF

The little river twittering in the twilight,
The wan, wondering look of the pale sky,
    This is almost bliss.

And everything shut up and gone to sleep,
All the troubles and anxieties and pain
    Gone under the twilight.

Only the twilight now, and the soft "Sh!" of the river
    That will last for ever.

And at last I know my love for you is here;
I can see it all, it is whole like the twilight,
It is large, so large, I could not see it before,
Because of the little lights and flickers and interruptions,
    Troubles, anxieties and pains.

    You are the call and I am the answer,
    You are the wish, and I the fulfilment,
    You are the night, and I the day.
        What else—it is perfect enough.
        It is perfectly complete,
        You and I,
        What more——?
Strange, how we suffer in spite of this.

LIGHTNING

I felt the lurch and halt of her heart
Next my breast, where my own heart was beating;
And I laughed to feel it plunge and bound,
And strange in my blood-swept ears was the sound
Of the words I kept repeating,
Repeating with tightened arms, and the hot blood's blindfold art.

Her breath flew warm against my neck,
    Warm as a flame in the close night air;
And the sense of her clinging flesh was sweet
Where her arms and my neck's blood-surge could meet.
    Holding her thus, did I care
That the black night hid her from me, blotted out every speck?

I leaned me forward to find her lips,
    And claim her utterly in a kiss,
When the lightning flew across her face,
And I saw her for the flaring space
    Of a second, afraid of the clips
Of my arms, inert with dread, wilted in fear of my kiss.

A moment, like a wavering spark,
    Her face lay there before my breast,
Pale love lost in a snow of fear,
And guarded by a glittering tear,
    And lips apart with dumb cries;
A moment, and she was taken again in the merciful dark.

I heard the thunder, and felt the rain,
    And my arms fell loose, and I was dumb.
Almost I hated her, she was so good.
Hated myself, and the place, and my blood,
    Which burned with rage, as I bade her come
Home, away home, ere the lightning floated forth again.

SONG-DAY IN AUTUMN

When the autumn roses
    Are heavy with dew,
Before the mist discloses
    The leaf's brown hue,
You would, among the laughing hills
    Of yesterday
Walk innocent in the daffodils,
Coiffing up your auburn hair
In a puritan fillet, a chaste white snare
To catch and keep me with you there
    So far away.

When from the autumn roses
    Trickles the dew,
When the blue mist uncloses
    And the sun looks through,
You from those startled hills
    Come away,
Out of the withering daffodils;
Thoughtful, and half afraid,
Plaiting a heavy, auburn braid
And coiling it round the wise brows of a maid
    Who was scared in her play.

When in the autumn roses
    Creeps a bee,
And a trembling flower encloses
    His ecstasy,
You from your lonely walk
    Turn away,
And leaning to me like a flower on its stalk,
Wait among the beeches
For your late bee who beseeches
To creep through your loosened hair till he reaches,
    Your heart of dismay.

AWARE

Slowly the moon is rising out of the ruddy haze,
Divesting herself of her golden shift, and so
Emerging white and exquisite; and I in amaze
See in the sky before me, a woman I did not know
I loved, but there she goes and her beauty hurts my heart;
I follow her down the night, begging her not to depart.

A PANG OF REMINISCENCE

High and smaller goes the moon, she is small and very far from me,
Wistful and candid, watching me wistfully, and I see
Trembling blue in her pallor a tear that surely I have seen before,
A tear which I had hoped that even hell held not again in store.

A WHITE BLOSSOM

A tiny moon as white and small as a single jasmine flower
Leans all alone above my window, on night's wintry bower,
Liquid as lime-tree blossom, soft as brilliant water or rain
She shines, the one white love of my youth, which all sin cannot stain.

RED MOON-RISE

The train in running across the weald has fallen into a steadier stroke
So even, it beats like silence, and sky and earth in one unbroke
Embrace of darkness lie around, and crushed between them all the
        loose
And littered lettering of leaves and hills and houses closed, and we can
        use
The open book of landscape no more, for the covers of darkness have
        shut upon
Its written pages, and sky and earth and all between are closed in one.

And we are smothered between the darkness, we close our eyes and say
        "Hush!" we try
To escape in sleep the terror of this immense deep darkness, and we lie
Wrapped up for sleep. And then, dear God, from out of the twofold
        darkness, red
As if from the womb the moon arises, as if the twin-walled darkness
        had bled
In one great spasm of birth and given us this new, red moon-rise
Which lies on the knees of the darkness bloody, and makes us hide our
        eyes.

The train beats frantic in haste, and struggles away
From this ruddy terror of birth that has slid down
From out of the loins of night to flame our way
With fear; but God, I am glad, so glad that I drown
My terror with joy of confirmation, for now
Lies God all red before me, and I am glad,
As the Magi were when they saw the rosy brow
Of the Infant bless their constant folly which had
Brought them thither to God: for now I know
That the Womb is a great red passion whence rises all
The shapeliness that decks us here-below:
Yea like the fire that boils within this ball
Of earth, and quickens all herself with flowers,
God burns within the stiffened clay of us;
And every flash of thought that we and ours
Send up to heaven, and every movement, does
Fly like a spark from this God-fire of passion;
And pain of birth, and joy of begetting,
And sweat of labour, and the meanest fashion
Of fretting or of gladness, but the jetting
Of a trail of the great fire against the sky
Where we can see it, a jet from the innermost fire:
And even in the watery shells that lie
Alive within the oozy under-mire,
A grain of this same fire I can descry.

And then within the screaming birds that fly
Across the lightning when the storm leaps higher;
And then the swirling, flaming folk that try
To come like fire-flames at their fierce desire,
They are as earth's dread, spurting flames that ply
Awhile and gush forth death and their expire.
And though it be love's wet blue eyes that cry
To hot love to relinquish its desire,
Still in their depths I see the same red spark
As rose tonight upon us from the dark.

RETURN

Now I am come again, you who have so desired
My coming, why do you look away from me?
Why does your cheek burn against me—have I inspired
Such anger as sets your mouth unwontedly?

Ah, here I sit while you break the music beneath
Your bow; for broken it is, and hurting to hear:
Cease then from music—does anguish of absence bequeath
Me only aloofness when I would draw near?

THE APPEAL

You, Helen, who see the stars
As mistletoe berries burning in a black tree,
You surely, seeing I am a bowl of kisses,
Should put your mouth to mine and drink of me.

Helen, you let my kisses steam
Wasteful into the night's black nostrils; drink
Me up I pray; oh you who are Night's Bacchante,
How can you from my bowl of kisses shrink!

REPULSED

The last, silk-floating thought has gone from the dandelion stem,
And the flesh of the stalk holds up for nothing a blank diadem.

The night's flood-winds have lifted my last desire from me.
And my hollow flesh stands up in the night abandonedly.

As I stand on this hill, with the whitening cave of the city beyond,
Helen, I am despoiled of my pride, and my soul turns fond:

Overhead the nightly heavens like an open, immense eye,
Like a cat's distended pupil sparkles with sudden stars.
As with thoughts that flash and crackle in uncouth malignancy
They glitter at me, and I fear the fierce snapping of night's thought-
    stars.

Beyond me, up the darkness, goes the gush of the lights of two towns,
As the breath which rushes upwards from the nostrils of an immense
Life crouched across the globe, ready, if need be, to pounce =
Across the space upon heaven's high hostile eminence.

All round me, but far away, the night's twin consciousness roars
With sounds that endlessly swell and sink like the storm of thought in
    the brain.
Lifting and falling like slow breaths taken, pulsing like oars
Immense that beat the blood of the night down its vein.

The night is immense and awful, Helen, and I am insect small
In the fur of this hill, clung on to the fur of shaggy, black heather.
A palpitant speck in the fur of the night, and afraid of all,
Seeing the world and the sky like creatures hostile together.

And I in the fur of the world, and you a pale fleck from the sky,
How we hate each other to-night, hate, you and I,
As the world of activity hates the dream that goes on on high,
As a man hates the dreaming woman he loves, but who will not reply.

DREAM-CONFUSED

Is that the moon
At the window so big and red?
No one in the room?
No one near the bed——?

Listen, her shoon
Palpitating down the stair?
—Or a beat of wings at the window there?

A moment ago
She kissed me warm on the mouth;
The very moon in the south
Is warm with a bloody glow;
The moon, from far abysses
Signalling those two kisses.

And now the moon
Goes slowly out of the west,
And slowly back in my breast
My kisses are sinking, soon
To leave me at rest.

COROT

The trees rise tall and taller, lifted
On a subtle rush of cool grey flame
That issuing out of the dawn has sifted
The spirit from each leaf's frame.

For the trailing, leisurely rapture of life
Drifts dimly forward, easily hidden
By bright leaves uttered aloud, and strife
Of shapes in the grey mist chidden.

The grey, phosphorescent, pellucid advance
Of the luminous purpose of God, shines out
Where the lofty trees athwart stream chance
    To shake flakes of its shadow about.

The subtle, steady rush of the whole
Grey foam-mist of advancing God,
As He silently sweeps to His somewhere, his goal,
    Is heard in the grass of the sod.

Is heard in the windless whisper of leaves
In the silent labours of men in the fields,
In the downward dropping of flimsy sheaves
    Of cloud the rain skies yield.

In the tapping haste of a fallen leaf,
In the flapping of red-roof smoke, and the small
Foot-stepping tap of men beneath
    These trees so huge and tall.

For what can all sharp-rimmed substance but catch
In a backward ripple, God's purpose, reveal
For a moment His mighty direction, snatch
    A spark beneath His wheel.

Since God sweeps onward dim and vast,
Creating the channelled vein of Man
And Leaf for His passage. His shadow is cast
    On all for us to scan.

Ah listen, for Silence is not lonely:
Imitate the magnificent trees
That speak no word of their rapture, but only
    Breathe largely the luminous breeze.

MORNING WORK

A gang of labourers on the piled wet timber
That shines blood-red beside the railway siding
Seem to be making out of the blue of the morning
Something faery and fine, the shuttles sliding,

The red-gold spools of their hands and faces shuttling
Hither and thither across the morn's crystalline frame
Of blue: trolls at the cave of ringing cerulean mining,
And laughing with work, living their work like a game.

TRANSFORMATIONS

I

The Town

Oh you stiff shapes, swift transformation seethes
About you: only last night you were
A Sodom smouldering in the dense, soiled air;
To-day a thicket of sunshine with blue smoke-wreaths.

To-morrow swimming in evening's vague, dim vapour
Like a weeded city in shadow under the sea,
Beneath an ocean of shimmering light you will be:
Then a group of toadstools waiting the moon's white taper.

And when I awake in the morning, after rain,
To find the new houses a cluster of lilies glittering
In scarlet, alive with the birds' bright twittering,
I'll say your bond of ugliness is vain.

II

The Earth

Oh Earth, you spinning clod of earth.
And then you lamp, you lemon-coloured beauty;
Oh Earth, you rotten apple rolling downward,
Then brilliant Earth, from the burr of night in beauty
As a jewel-brown horse-chestnut newly issued:—
You are all these, and strange, it is my duty
To take you all, sordid or radiant tissued.

III

Men

Oh labourers, oh shuttles across the blue frame of morning,
You feet of the rainbow balancing the sky!
Oh you who flash your arms like rockets to heaven,
Who in lassitude lean as yachts on the sea-wind lie!
You who in crowds are rhododendrons in blossom,
Who stand alone in pride like lighted lamps;
Who grappling down with work or hate or passion.
Take strange lithe form of a beast that sweats and ramps:
You who are twisted in grief like crumpled beech-leaves,
Who curl in sleep like kittens, who kiss as a swarm
Of clustered, vibrating bees; who fall to earth

At last like a bean-pod: what are you, oh multiform?

RENASCENCE

We have bit no forbidden apple,
    Eve and I,
Yet the splashes of day and night
Falling round us no longer dapple
The same Eden with purple and white.

This is our own still valley
    Our Eden, our home,
But day shows it vivid with feeling
And the pallor of night does not tally
With dark sleep that once covered its ceiling.

My little red heifer, to-night I looked in her eyes,
    —She will calve to-morrow:
Last night when I went with the lantern, the sow was grabbing her litter
With red, snarling jaws: and I heard the cries
Of the new-born, and after that, the old owl, then the bats that flitter.

And I woke to the sound of the wood-pigeons, and lay and listened,
    Till I could borrow
A few quick beats of a wood-pigeon's heart, and when I did rise
The morning sun on the shaken iris glistened,
And I saw that home, this valley, was wider than Paradise.

I learned it all from my Eve
    This warm, dumb wisdom.
She's a finer instructress than years;
She has taught my heart-strings to weave
Through the web of all laughter and tears.

And now I see the valley
    Fleshed all like me
With feelings that change and quiver:
And all things seem to tally
    With something in me,
Something of which she's the giver.

DOG-TIRED

If she would come to me here
    Now the sunken swaths
    Are glittering paths
To the sun, and the swallows cut clear
Into the setting sun! if she came to me here!

If she would come to me now,
Before the last-mown harebells are dead;
While that vetch-clump still burns red!
Before all the bats have dropped from the bough
To cool in the night; if she came to me now!

The horses are untackled, the chattering machine
Is still at last. If she would come
We could gather up the dry hay from
The hill-brow, and lie quite still, till the green
Sky ceased to quiver, and lost its active sheen.

I should like to drop
On the hay, with my head on her knee,
And lie dead still, while she
Breathed quiet above me; and the crop
Of stars grew silently.

I should like to lie still
As if I was dead; but feeling
Her hand go stealing
Over my face and my head, until
This ache was shed.

MICHAEL-ANGELO

God shook thy roundness in His finger's cup,
He sunk His hands in firmness down thy sides,
And drew the circle of His grasp, O Man,
Along thy limbs delighted, thine, His bride's.

And so thou wert God-shapen: His finger
Curved thy mouth for thee, and His strong shoulder
Planted thee upright: art not proud to see
In the curve of thine exquisite form the joy of the Moulder?

He took a handful of light and rolled a ball,
Compressed it till its beam grew wondrous dark,
Then gave thee thy dark eyes, O Man, that all
He made had doorway to thee through that spark.

God, lonely, put down His mouth in a kiss of creation,
He kissed thee, O Man, in a passion of love, and left
The vivid life of His love in thy mouth and thy nostrils;
Keep then the kiss from the adultress' theft.

VIOLETS

Sister, tha knows while we was on the planks
   Aside o' th' grave, while th' coffin wor lyin' yet
On th' yaller clay, an' th' white flowers top of it
   Tryin' to keep off'n him a bit o' th' wet,

An' parson makin' haste, an' a' the black
   Huddlin' close together a cause o' th' rain,
Did t' 'appen ter notice a bit of a lass away back
   By a head-stun, sobbin' an' sobbin' again?

    —How should I be lookin' round
      An' me standin' on the plank
    Beside the open ground,
      Where our Ted 'ud soon be sank?

    Yi, an' 'im that young,
      Snapped sudden out of all
    His wickedness, among
      Pals worse n'r ony name as you could call.

Let be that; there's some o' th' bad as we
   Like better nor all your good, an' 'e was one.
—And cos I liked him best, yi, bett'r nor thee,
   I canna bide to think where he is gone.

Ah know tha liked 'im bett'r nor me. But let
   Me tell thee about this lass. When you had gone
Ah stopped behind on t' pad i' th' drippin' wet
   An' watched what 'er 'ad on.

Tha should ha' seed her slive up when we'd gone,
   Tha should ha' seed her kneel an' look in
At th' sloppy wet grave—an' 'er little neck shone
   That white, an' 'er shook that much, I'd like to begin

Scraïghtin' my-sen as well. 'En undid her black
   Jacket at th' bosom, an' took from out of it
Over a double 'andful of violets, all in a pack
   Ravelled blue and white—warm, for a bit

O' th' smell come waftin' to me. 'Er put 'er face
   Right intil 'em and scraïghted out again,
Then after a bit 'er dropped 'em down that place,
   An' I come away, because o' the teemin' rain.

WHETHER OR NOT

I

Dunna thee tell me its his'n, mother,
     Dunna thee, dunna thee.
—Oh ay! he'll be comin' to tell thee his-sen
     Wench, wunna he?

Tha doesna mean to say to me, mother,
     He's gone wi that—
—My gel, owt'll do for a man i' the dark,
     Tha's got it flat.

But 'er's old, mother, 'er's twenty year
     Older nor him—
—Ay, an' yaller as a crowflower, an' yet i' the dark
     Er'd do for Tim.

Tha niver believes it, mother, does ter?
     It's somebody's lies.
—Ax him thy-sen wench—a widder's lodger;
     It's no surprise.

II

A widow of forty-five
With a bitter, swarthy skin,
To ha' 'ticed a lad o' twenty-five
An' 'im to have been took in!

A widow of forty-five
As has sludged like a horse all her life,
Till 'er's tough as whit-leather, to slive
Atween a lad an' 'is wife!

A widow at forty-five,
A tough old otchel wi' long
Witch teeth, an' 'er black hawk-eyes as I've
Mistrusted all along!

An' me as 'as kep my-sen
Shut like a daisy bud,
Clean an' new an' nice, so's when
He wed he'd ha'e summat good!

An' 'im as nice an' fresh
As any man i' the force,
To ha'e gone an' given his white young flesh
To a woman that coarse!

III

You're stout to brave this snow, Miss Stainwright,
    Are you makin' Brinsley way?
—I'm off up th' line to Underwood
    Wi' a dress as is wanted to-day.

Oh are you goin' to Underwood?
    'Appen then you've 'eered?
—What's that as 'appen I've 'eered-on, Missis,
    Speak up, you nedna be feared.

Why, your young man an' Widow Naylor,
    Her as he lodges wi',
They say he's got her wi' childt; but there,
    It's nothing to do wi' me.

Though if it's true they'll turn him out
    O' th' p'lice force, without fail;
An' if it's not true, I'd back my life
    They'll listen to *her* tale.

Well, I'm believin' no tale, Missis,
    I'm seein' for my-sen;
An' when I know for sure, Missis,
    I'll talk *then*.

IV

Nay robin red-breast, tha nedna
    Sit noddin' thy head at me;
My breast's as red as thine, I reckon,
    Flayed red, if tha could but see.

Nay, you blessed pee-whips,
    You nedna screet at me!
I'm screetin' my-sen, but are-na goin'
    To let iv'rybody see.

Tha *art* smock-ravelled, bunny,
    Larropin' neck an' crop
I' th' snow: but I's warrant thee, bunny,
    I'm further ower th' top.

V

Now sithee theer at th' railroad crossin'
Warmin' his-sen at the stool o' fire
Under the tank as fills the ingines,
If there isn't any dearly-beloved liar!

My constable wi' 'is buttoned breast
As stout as the truth, my sirs!—An' 'is face
As bold as a robin! It's much he cares
For this nice old shame and disgrace.

Oh but he drops his flag when 'e sees me,
Yes, an' 'is face goes white ... oh yes
Tha can stare at me wi' thy fierce blue eyes,
But tha doesna stare me out, I guess!

VI

Whativer brings thee out so far
    In a' this depth o' snow?
—I'm takin' 'ome a weddin' dress
    If tha maun know.

Why, is there a weddin' at Underwood,
    As tha ne'd trudge up here?
—It's Widow Naylor's weddin'-dress,
    An' 'er's wantin it, I hear.

'Er doesna want no weddin'-dress . . .
    What—but what dost mean?
—Doesn't ter know what I mean, Tim?—Yi,
    Tha must' a' been hard to wean!

Tha'rt a good-un at suckin-in yet, Timmy;
    But tell me, isn't it true
As 'er'll be wantin' my weddin'-dress
    In a week or two?

Tha's no occasions ter ha'e me on
    Lizzie—what's done is done!—
—*Done*, I should think so—Done! But might
    I ask when tha begun?

It's thee as 'as done it as much as me,
    Lizzie, I tell thee that.
—"Me gotten a childt to thy landlady—!"
    Tha's gotten thy answer pat,

As tha allers hast—but let me tell thee
    Hasna ter sent me whoam, when I
Was a'most burstin' mad o' my-sen
    An' walkin' in agony;

After thy kisses, Lizzie, after
    Tha's lain right up to me Lizzie, an' melted
Into me, melted into me, Lizzie,
    Till I was verily swelted.

An' if my landlady seed me like it,
    An 'if 'er clawkin', tiger's eyes
Went through me just as the light went out
    Is it any cause for surprise?

No cause for surprise at all, my lad,
    After lickin' and snuffin' at me, tha could
Turn thy mouth on a woman like her—
    Did ter find her good?

Ay, I did, but afterwards
    I should like to ha' killed her!
—Afterwards!—an' after how long
    Wor it tha'd liked to 'a killed her?

Say no more, Liz, dunna thee,
    I might lose my-sen.
—I'll only say good-bye to thee, Timothy,
    An' gi'e her thee back again.

I'll ta'e thy word "Good-bye," Liz,
    But I shonna marry her,
I shonna for nobody.—It is
    Very nice, on you, Sir.

The childt maun ta'e its luck, it maun,
    An' she maun ta'e her luck,
For I tell ye I shonna marry her—
    What her's got, her took.

That's spoken like a man, Timmy,
    That's spoken like a man . . .
"He up an' fired off his pistol
    An' then away he ran."

I damn well shanna marry 'er,
    So chew at it no more,
Or I'll chuck the flamin' lot of you—
    —You nedn't have swore.

VII

That's his collar round the candle-stick
An' that's the dark blue tie I bought 'im,
An' these is the woman's kids he's so fond on,
An' 'ere comes the cat that caught 'im.

I dunno where his eyes was—a gret
Round-shouldered hag! My sirs, to think
Of him stoopin' to her! You'd wonder he could
Throw hisself in that sink.

I expect you know who I am, Mrs. Naylor!
    —Who yer are?—yis, you're Lizzie Stainwright.
'An 'appen you might guess what I've come for?
    —'Appen I mightn't, 'appen I might.

You knowed as I was courtin' Tim Merfin.
    —Is, I knowed 'e wor courtin' thee.
An' yet you've been carryin' on wi' him.
    —Ay, an' 'im wi' me.

Well, now you've got to pay for it,
    —An' if I han, what's that to thee?
For 'e isn't goin' to marry you.
    —Is it a toss-up 'twixt thee an' me?

It's no toss-up 'twixt thee an' me.
    —Then what art colleyfoglin' for?
I'm not havin' your orts an' slarts.
    —Which on us said you wor?

I want you to know 'e's non marryin' you.
   —Tha wants 'im thy-sen too bad.
Though I'll see as 'e pays you, an' comes to the scratch.
   —Tha'rt for doin' a lot wi' th' lad.

VIII

To think I should ha'e to haffle an' caffle
   Wi' a woman, an' pay 'er a price
For lettin' me marry the lad as I thought
   To marry wi' cabs an' rice.

But we'll go unbeknown to the registrar,
   An' give *'er* what money there is,
For I won't be beholden to such as her
   For anythink of his.

IX

Take off thy duty stripes, Tim,
   An' come wi' me in here,
Ta'e off thy p'lice-man's helmet
   An' look me clear.

I wish tha hadna done it, Tim,
   I do, an' that I do!
For whenever I look thee i' th' face, I s'll see
   Her face too.

I wish tha could wesh 'er off'n thee,
   For I used to think that thy
Face was the finest thing that iver
   Met my eye. . . .

X

Twenty pounds o' thy own tha hast, and fifty pound ha'e I,
Thine shall go to pay the woman, an' wi' my bit we'll buy
All as we shall want for furniture when tha leaves this place,
An' we'll be married at th' registrar—now lift thy face.

Lift thy face an' look at me, man, up an' look at me:
Sorry I am for this business, an' sorry if I ha'e driven thee
To such a thing: but it's a poor tale, that I'm bound to say,
Before I can ta'e thee I've got a widow of forty-five to pay.

Dunnat thee think but what I love thee—I love thee well,
But 'deed an' I wish as this tale o' thine wor niver my tale to tell;
Deed an' I wish as I could stood at the altar wi' thee an' been proud o'
    thee,
That I could ha' been first woman to thee, as thou'rt first man to me.

But we maun ma'e the best on't—I'll rear thy childt if 'er'll yield it to
    me,
An' then wi' that twenty pound we gi'e 'er I s'd think 'er wunna be
So very much worser off than 'er wor before—An' now look up
An' answer me—for I've said my say, an' there's no more sorrow to sup.

Yi, tha'rt a man, tha'rt a fine big man, but niver a baby had eyes
As sulky an' ormin' as thine. Hast owt to say otherwise
From what I've arranged wi' thee? Eh man, what a stubborn jackass
    thou art,
Kiss me then—there—ne'er mind if I scraight—I wor fond o' thee,
    Sweetheart.

A COLLIER'S WIFE

Somebody's knocking at the door
    Mother, come down and see.
—I's think it's nobbut a beggar,
    Say I'm busy.

It's not a beggar, mother,—hark
    How hard he knocks . . .
—Eh, tha'rt a mard-'arsed kid,
    'E'll gi'e thee socks!

Shout an' ax what 'e wants,
    I canna come down.
—'E says "Is it Arthur Holliday's?"
    Say "Yes," tha clown.

'E says, "Tell your mother as 'er mester's
    Got hurt i' th' pit."
What—oh my sirs, 'e never says that,
    That's niver it.

Come out o' the way an' let me see,
    Eh, there's no peace!
An' stop thy scraightin', childt,
    Do shut thy face.

"Your mester's 'ad an accident,
    An' they're ta'ein 'im i' th' ambulance
To Nottingham,"—Eh, dear o' me
    If 'e's not a man for mischance!

Wheers he hurt this time, lad?
    —I dunna know,
They on'y towd me it wor bad—
    It would be so!

Eh, what a man!—an' that cobbly road,
    They'll jolt him a'most to death,
I'm sure he's in for some trouble
    Nigh every time he takes breath.

Out o' my way, childt—dear o' me, wheer
    Have I put his clean stockings and shirt;
Goodness knows if they'll be able
    To take off his pit dirt.

An' what a moan he'll make—there niver
    Was such a man for a fuss
If anything ailed him—at any rate
    I shan't have him to nuss.

I do hope it's not very bad!
    Eh, what a shame it seems
As some should ha'e hardly a smite o' trouble
    An' others has reams.

It's a shame as 'e should be knocked about
    Like this, I'm sure it is!
He's had twenty accidents, if he's had one;
    Owt bad, an' it's his.

There's one thing, we'll have peace for a bit,
    Thank Heaven for a peaceful house;
An' there's compensation, sin' it's accident,
    An' club money—I nedn't grouse.

An' a fork an' a spoon he'll want, an' what else;
    I s'll never catch that train—
What a trapse it is if a man gets hurt—
    I s'd think he'll get right again.

THE DRAINED CUP

The snow is witherin' off n th' gress
    Love, should I tell thee summat?
The snow is witherin' off'n th' gress
An' a thick mist sucks at the clots o' snow,
An' the moon above in a weddin' dress
Goes fogged an' slow—
    Love, should I tell thee summat?

Tha's been snowed up i' this cottage wi' me,
    Nay, I'm tellin' thee summat.—
Tha's bin snowed up i' this cottage wi' me
While th' clocks has a' run down an' stopped
An' the short days withering silently
Unbeknown have dropped.
    —Yea, but I'm tellin' thee summat.

How many days dost think has gone?—
    Now I'm tellin' thee summat.
How many days dost think has gone?
How many days has the candle-light shone
On us as tha got more white an' wan?
—Seven days, or none—
    Am I not tellin' thee summat?

Tha come to bid farewell to me—
    Tha'rt frit o' summat.
To kiss me and shed a tear wi' me,
Then off and away wi' the weddin' ring
For the girl who was grander, and better than me
For marrying—
    Tha'rt frit o' summat?

I durstna kiss thee tha trembles so,
    Tha'rt frit o' summat.
Tha arena very flig to go,
'Appen the mist from the thawin' snow
Daunts thee—it isna for love, I know,
That tha'rt loath to go.
    —Dear o' me, say summat.

Maun tha cling to the wa' as tha goes,
      So bad as that?
Tha'lt niver get into thy weddin' clothes
At that rate—eh, theer goes thy hat;
Ne'er mind, good-bye lad, now I lose
My joy, God knows,
      —An' worse nor that.

The road goes under the apple tree;
      Look, for I'm showin' thee summat.
An' if it worn't for the mist, tha'd see
The great black wood on all sides o' thee
Wi' the little pads going cunningly
To ravel thee.
      So listen, I'm tellin' thee summat.

When tha comes to the beechen avenue,
      I'm warnin' thee o' summat.
Mind tha shall keep inwards, a few
Steps to the right, for the gravel pits
Are steep an' deep wi' watter, an' you
Are scarce o' your wits.
      Remember, I've warned thee o' summat.

An' mind when crossin' the planken bridge,
      Again I warn ye o' summat.
Ye slip not on the slippery ridge
Of the thawin' snow, or it'll be
A long put-back to your gran' marridge,
I'm tellin' ye.
      Nay, are ter scared o' summat?

In kep the thick black curtains drawn,
      Am I not tellin' thee summat?
Against the knockin' of sevenfold dawn,
An 'red-tipped candles from morn to morn
Have dipped an' danced upon thy brawn
Till thou art worn—
      Oh, I have cost thee summat.

Look in the mirror an' see thy-sen,
      —What, I am showin' thee summat.
Wasted an' wan tha sees thy-sen,
An' thy hand that holds the mirror shakes
Till tha drops the glass and tha shoulders when
Thy luck breaks.
      Sure, tha'rt afraid o' summat.

Frail thou art, my saucy man,
    —Listen, I'm tellin' thee summat.
Tottering and tired thou art, my man,
Tha came to say good-bye to me,
An' tha's done it so well, that now I can
Part wi' thee.
    —Master, I'm givin' thee s summat.

THE SCHOOLMASTER

I

A SNOWY DAY IN SCHOOL

All the slow school hours, round the irregular hum of the class,
Have pressed immeasurable spaces of hoarse silence
Muffling my mind, as snow muffles the sounds that pass
Down the soiled street. We have pattered the lessons ceaselessly—
But the faces of the boys, in the brooding, yellow light
Have shone for me like a crowded constellation of stars,
Like full-blown flowers dimly shaking at the night,
Like floating froth on an ebbing shore in the moon.

Out of each star, dark, strange beams that disquiet:
In the open depths of each flower, dark restless drops:
Twin bubbles, shadow-full of mystery and challenge in the foam's
       whispering riot:
—How can I answer the challenge of so many eyes!

The thick snow is crumpled on the roof, it plunges down
Awfully. Must I call back those hundred eyes?—
A voice
Wakes from the hum, faltering about a noun—
My question! My God, I must break from this hoarse silence

That rustles beyond the stars to me.—There,
I have startled a hundred eyes, and I must look
Them an answer back. It is more than I can bear.
The snow descends as if the dull sky shook
In flakes of shadow down; and through the gap
Between the ruddy schools sweeps one black rook.

The rough snowball in the playground stands huge and still
With fair flakes settling down on it.—Beyond, the town
Is lost in the shadowed silence the skies distil.
And all things are possessed by silence, and they can brood
Wrapped up in the sky's dim space of hoarse silence
Earnestly—and oh for me this class is a bitter rood.

II

THE BEST OF SCHOOL

The blinds are drawn because of the sun,
And the boys and the room in a colourless gloom
Of under-water float: bright ripples run
Across the walls as the blinds are blown
To let the sunlight in; and I,
As I sit on the beach of the class alone,
Watch the boys in their summer blouses,
As they write, their round heads busily bowed:
And one after another rouses
And lifts his face and looks at me,
And my eyes meet his very quietly,
Then he turns again to his work, with glee.

With glee he turns, with a little glad
Ecstasy of work he turns from me,
An ecstasy surely sweet to be had.
And very sweet while the sunlight waves
In the fresh of the morning, it is to be
A teacher of these young boys, my slaves
Only as swallows are slaves to the eaves
They build upon, as mice are slaves
To the man who threshes and sows the sheaves.

Oh, sweet it is
To feel the lads' looks light on me,
Then back in a swift, bright flutter to work,
As birds who are stealing turn and flee.

Touch after touch I feel on me
As their eyes glance at me for the grain
Of rigour they taste delightedly.

And all the class,
As tendrils reached out yearningly
Slowly rotate till they touch the tree
That they cleave unto, that they leap along
Up to their lives—so they to me.

So do they cleave and cling to me,
So I lead them up, so do they twine
Me up, caress and clothe with free
Fine foliage of lives this life of mine;
The lowest stem of this life of mine,
The old hard stem of my life
That bears aloft towards rarer skies
My top of life, that buds on high
Amid the high wind's enterprise.
They all do clothe my ungrowing life
With a rich, a thrilled young clasp of life;
A clutch of attachment, like parenthood,
Mounts up to my heart, and I find it good.

And I lift my head upon the troubled tangled world, and though the
        pain
Of living my life were doubled, I still have this to comfort and sustain,
I have such swarming sense of lives at the base of me, such sense of
        lives
Clustering upon me, reaching up, as each after the other strives
To follow my life aloft to the fine wild air of life and the storm of
        thought,
And though I scarcely see the boys, or know that they are there,
        distraught

As I am with living my life in earnestness, still progressively and alone,
Though they cling, forgotten the most part, not companions, scarcely
        known
To me—yet still because of the sense of their closeness clinging
        densely to me,
And slowly fingering up my stem and following all tinily
The way that I have gone and now am leading, they are dear to me.

They keep me assured, and when my soul feels lonely,
All mistrustful of thrusting its shoots where only
I alone am living, then it keeps
Me comforted to feel the warmth that creeps
Up dimly from their striving; it heartens my strife:
And when my heart is chill with loneliness,
Then comforts it the creeping tenderness
Of all the strays of life that climb my life.

III

AFTERNOON IN SCHOOL

THE LAST LESSON

When will the bell ring, and end this weariness?
How long have they tugged the leash, and strained apart
My pack of unruly hounds: I cannot start
Them again on a quarry of knowledge they hate to hunt,
I can haul them and urge them no more.
No more can I endure to bear the brunt
Of the books that lie out on the desks: a full three score
Of several insults of blotted pages and scrawl
Of slovenly work that they have offered me.
I am sick, and tired more than any thrall
Upon the woodstacks working wcariedly.

        And shall I take
The last dear fuel and heap it on my soul
Till I rouse my will like a fire to consume
Their dross of indifference, and burn the scroll
Of their insults in punishment?—I will not!
I will not waste myself to embers for them,
Not all for them shall the fires of my life be hot.
For myself a heap of ashes of weariness, till sleep
Shall have raked the embers clear: I will keep
Some of my strength for myself, for if I should sell
It all for them, I should hate them—
       —I will sit and wait for the bell.

AMORES (1916)

TO
OTTOLINE MORRELL
IN TRIBUTE
TO HER NOBLE
AND INDEPENDENT SYMPATHY
AND HER GENEROUS UNDERSTANDING
THESE POEMS
ARE GRATEFULLY DEDICATED

TEASE

I will give you all my keys,
  You shall be my châtelaine,
You shall enter as you please,
  As you please shall go again.

When I hear you jingling through
  All the chambers of my soul,
How I sit and laugh at you
  In your vain housekeeping rôle.

Jealous of the smallest cover,
  Angry at the simplest door;
Well, you anxious, inquisitive lover,
  Are you pleased with what's in store?

You have fingered all my treasures,
  Have you not, most curiously,
Handled all my tools and measures
  And masculine machinery?

Over every single beauty
  You have had your little rapture;
You have slain, as was your duty,
  Every sin-mouse you could capture.

Still you are not satisfied,
  Still you tremble faint reproach;
Challenge me I keep aside
  Secrets that you may not broach.

Maybe yes, and maybe no,
  Maybe there are secret places,
Altars barbarous below,
  Elsewhere halls of high disgraces.

Maybe yes, and maybe no,
   You may have it as you please,
Since I choose to keep you so,
   Suppliant on your curious knees.

THE WILD COMMON

The quick sparks on the gorse bushes are leaping,
Little jets of sunlight-texture imitating flame;
Above them, exultant, the pee-wits are sweeping:
They are lords of the desolate wastes of sadness their screamings
    proclaim.

Rabbits, handfuls of brown earth, lie
Low-rounded on the mournful grass they have bitten down to the quick.
Are they asleep?—Are they alive?—Now see, when I
Move my arms the hill bursts and heaves under their spurting kick.

The common flaunts bravely; but below, from the rushes
Crowds of glittering king-cups surge to challenge the blossoming
    bushes;
There the lazy streamlet pushes
Its curious course mildly; here it wakes again, leaps, laughs, and
    gushes.

Into a deep pond, an old sheep-dip,
Dark, overgrown with willows, cool, with the brook ebbing through so
    slow,
Naked on the steep, soft lip
Of the bank I stand watching my own white shadow quivering to and
    fro.

What if the gorse flowers shrivelled and kissing were lost?
Without the pulsing waters, where were the marigolds and the songs of
    the brook?
If my veins and my breasts with love embossed
Withered, my insolent soul would be gone like flowers that the hot
    wind took.

So my soul like a passionate woman turns,
Filled with remorseful terror to the man she scorned, and her love
For myself in my own eyes' laughter burns,
Runs ecstatic over the pliant folds rippling down to my belly from the
    breast-lights above.

Over my sunlit skin the warm, clinging air,
Rich with the songs of seven larks singing at once, goes kissing me
      glad.
And the soul of the wind and my blood compare
Their wandering happiness, and the wind, wasted in liberty, drifts on
      and is sad.

Oh but the water loves me and folds me,
Plays with me, sways me, lifts me and sinks me as though it were living
      blood,
Blood of a heaving woman who holds me,
Owning my supple body a rare glad thing, supremely good.

STUDY

Somewhere the long mellow note of the blackbird
Quickens the unclasping hands of hazel,
Somewhere the wind-flowers fling their heads back,
Stirred by an impetuous wind. Some ways'll
All be sweet with white and blue violet.
    (*Hush now, hush. Where am I?—Biuret—*)

On the green wood's edge a shy girl hovers
From out of the hazel-screen on to the grass,
Where wheeling and screaming the petulant plovers
Wave frighted. Who comes? A labourer, alas!
Oh the sunset swims in her eyes' swift pool.
    (*Work, work, you fool—!*)

Somewhere the lamp hanging low from the ceiling
Lights the soft hair of a girl as she reads,
And the red firelight steadily wheeling
Weaves the hard hands of my friend in sleep.
And the white dog snuffs the warmth, appealing
For the man to heed lest the girl shall weep.

(*Tears and dreams for them; for me*
Bitter science—the exams. are near.
I wish I bore it more patiently.
I wish you did not wait, my dear,
For me to come: since work I must:
Though it's all the same when we are dead.—
I wish I was only a bust,
    All head.)

DISCORD IN CHILDHOOD

Outside the house an ash-tree hung its terrible whips,
And at night when the wind arose, the lash of the tree
Shrieked and slashed the wind, as a ship's
Weird rigging in a storm shrieks hideously.

Within the house two voices arose in anger, a slender lash
Whistling delirious rage, and the dreadful sound
Of a thick lash booming and bruising, until it drowned
The other voice in a silence of blood, 'neath the noise of the ash.

VIRGIN YOUTH

Now and again
All my body springs alive,
And the life that is polarised in my eyes,
That quivers between my eyes and mouth,
Flies like a wild thing across my body,
Leaving my eyes half-empty, and clamorous,
Filling my still breasts with a flush and a flame,
Gathering the soft ripples below my breasts
Into urgent, passionate waves,
And my soft, slumbering belly
Quivering awake with one impulse of desire,
Gathers itself fiercely together;
And my docile, fluent arms
Knotting themselves with wild strength
To clasp what they have never clasped.
Then I tremble, and go trembling
Under the wild, strange tyranny of my body,
Till it has spent itself,
And the relentless nodality of my eyes reasserts itself,
Till the bursten flood of life ebbs back to my eyes,
Back from my beautiful, lonely body
Tired and unsatisfied.

MONOLOGUE OF A MOTHER

This is the last of all, this is the last!
I must hold my hands, and turn my face to the fire,
I must watch my dead days fusing together in dross,
Shape after shape, and scene after scene from my past
Fusing to one dead mass in the sinking fire
Where the ash on the dying coals grows swiftly, like heavy moss.

Strange he is, my son, whom I have awaited like a lover,
Strange to me like a captive in a foreign country, haunting
The confines and gazing out on the land where the wind is free;
White and gaunt, with wistful eyes that hover
Always on the distance, as if his soul were chaunting
The monotonous weird of departure away from me.

Like a strange white bird blown out of the frozen seas,
Like a bird from the far north blown with a broken wing
Into our sooty garden, he drags and beats
From place to place perpetually, seeking release
From me, from the hand of my love which creeps up, needing
His happiness, whilst he in displeasure retreats.

I must look away from him, for my faded eyes
Like a cringing dog at his heels offend him now,
Like a toothless hound pursuing him with my will,
Till he chafes at my crouching persistence, and a sharp spark flies
In my soul from under the sudden frown of his brow,
As he blenches and turns away, and my heart stands still.

This is the last, it will not be any more.
All my life I have borne the burden of myself,
All the long years of sitting in my husband's house,
Never have I said to myself as he closed the door:
"Now I am caught!—You are hopelessly lost, O Self,
You are frightened with joy, my heart, like a frightened mouse."

Three times have I offered myself, three times rejected.
It will not be any more. No more, my son, my son!
Never to know the glad freedom of obedience, since long ago
The angel of childhood kissed me and went. I expected
Another would take me,—and now, my son, O my son,
I must sit awhile and wait, and never know
The loss of myself, till death comes, who cannot fail.

Death, in whose service is nothing of gladness, takes me;
For the lips and the eyes of God are behind a veil.
And the thought of the lipless voice of the Father shakes me
With fear, and fills my eyes with the tears of desire,
And my heart rebels with anguish as night draws nigher,

IN A BOAT

See the stars, love,
In the water much clearer and brighter
Than those above us, and whiter,
Like nenuphars.

Star-shadows shine, love,
How many stars in your bowl?
How many shadows in your soul,
Only mine, love, mine?

When I move the oars, love,
See how the stars are tossed,
Distorted, the brightest lost.
—So that bright one of yours, love.

The poor waters spill
The stars, waters broken, forsaken.
—The heavens are not shaken, you say, love,
Its stars stand still.

There, did you see
That spark fly up at us; even
Stars are not safe in heaven.
—What of yours, then, love, yours?

What then, love, if soon
Your light be tossed over a wave?
Will you count the darkness a grave,
And swoon, love, swoon?

WEEK-NIGHT SERVICE

The five old bells
Are hurrying and eagerly calling,
Imploring, protesting
They know, but clamorously falling
Into gabbling incoherence, never resting,
Like spattering showers from a bursten sky-rocket dropping
In splashes of sound, endlessly, never stopping.

The silver moon
That somebody has spun so high
To settle the question, yes or no, has caught
In the net of the night's balloon,
And sits with a smooth bland smile up there in the sky

Smiling at naught,
Unless the winking star that keeps her company
Makes little jests at the bells' insanity,
As if he knew aught!

The patient Night
Sits indifferent, hugged in her rags,
She neither knows nor cares
Why the old church sobs and brags;
The light distresses her eyes, and tears
Her old blue cloak, as she crouches and covers her face,
Smiling, perhaps, if we knew it, at the bells' loud clattering disgrace.

The wise old trees
Drop their leaves with a faint, sharp hiss of contempt,
While a car at the end of the street goes by with a laugh;
As by degrees
The poor bells cease, and the Night is exempt,
And the stars can chaff
The ironic moon at their ease, while the dim old church
Is peopled with shadows and sounds and ghosts that lurch
In its cenotaph.

IRONY

Always, sweetheart,
Carry into your room the blossoming boughs of cherry,
Almond and apple and pear diffuse with light, that very
Soon strews itself on the floor; and keep the radiance of spring
Fresh quivering; keep the sunny-swift March-days waiting
In a little throng at your door, and admit the one who is plaiting
Her hair for womanhood, and play awhile with her, then bid her depart.

A come and go of March-day loves
Through the flower-vine, trailing screen;
    A fluttering in of doves.
Then a launch abroad of shrinking doves
Over the waste where no hope is seen
Of open hands:

            Dance in and out
Small-bosomed girls of the spring of love,
With a bubble of laughter, and shrilly shout
Of mirth; then the dripping of tears on your glove.

DREAMS OLD AND NASCENT

OLD

I have opened the window to warm my hands on the sill
Where the sunlight soaks in the stone: the afternoon
Is full of dreams, my love, the boys are all still
In a wistful dream of Lorna Doone.

The clink of the shunting engines is sharp and fine,
Like savage music striking far off, and there
On the great, uplifted blue palace, lights stir and shine
Where the glass is domed in the blue, soft air.

There lies the world, my darling, full of wonder and wistfulness and
        strange
Recognition and greetings of half-acquaint things, as
I greet the cloud
Of blue palace aloft there, among misty indefinite dreams that range
At the back of my life's horizon, where the dreaming of past lives
        crowd.

Over the nearness of Norwood Hill, through the mellow veil
Of the afternoon glows to me the old romance of David and Dora,
With the old, sweet, soothing tears, and laughter that shakes the sail
Of the ship of the soul over seas where dreamed dreams lure the
        unoceaned explorer.

All the bygone, hushèd years
Streaming back where the mist distils
Into forgetfulness: soft-sailing waters where fears
No longer shake, where the silk sail fills
With an unfelt breeze that ebbs over the seas, where the storm
Of living has passed, on and on
Through the coloured iridescence that swims in the warm
Wake of the tumult now spent and gone,
Drifts my boat, wistfully lapsing after
The mists of vanishing tears and the echo of laughter.

DREAMS OLD AND NASCENT

NASCENT

My world is a painted fresco, where coloured shapes
Of old, ineffectual lives linger blurred and warm;
An endless tapestry the past has woven drapes
The halls of my life, compelling my soul to conform.

The surface of dreams is broken,
The picture of the past is shaken and scattered.
Fluent, active figures of men pass along the railway, and I am woken
From the dreams that the distance flattered.

Along the railway, active figures of men.
They have a secret that stirs in their limbs as they move
Out of the distance, nearer, commanding my dreamy world.

Here in the subtle, rounded flesh
Beats the active ecstasy.
In the sudden lifting my eyes, it is clearer,
The fascination of the quick, restless Creator moving through the mesh
Of men, vibrating in ecstasy through the rounded flesh.

Oh my boys, bending over your books,
In you is trembling and fusing
The creation of a new-patterned dream, dream of a generation:
And I watch to see the Creator, the power that patterns the dream.

The old dreams are beautiful, beloved, soft-toned, and sure,
But the dream-stuff is molten and moving mysteriously,
Alluring my eyes; for I, am I not also dream-stuff,
Am I not quickening, diffusing myself in the pattern, shaping and
    shapen?

Here in my class is the answer for the great yearning:
Eyes where I can watch the swim of old dreams reflected on the molten
    metal of dreams,
Watch the stir which is rhythmic and moves them all as a heart-beat
    moves the blood,
Here in the swelling flesh the great activity working,
Visible there in the change of eyes and the mobile features.

Oh the great mystery and fascination of the unseen Shaper,
The power of the melting, fusing Force—heat, light, all in one,
Everything great and mysterious in one, swelling and shaping the
    dream in the flesh,
As it swells and shapes a bud into blossom.

Oh the terrible ecstasy of the consciousness that I am life!
Oh the miracle of the whole, the widespread, labouring concentration
Swelling mankind like one bud to bring forth the fruit of a dream,
Oh the terror of lifting the innermost I out of the sweep of the impulse
    of life,
And watching the great Thing labouring through the whole round flesh
    of the world;

And striving to catch a glimpse of the shape of the coming dream,
As it quickens within the labouring, white-hot metal,
Catch the scent and the colour of the coming dream,
Then to fall back exhausted into the unconscious, molten life!

A WINTER'S TALE

Yesterday the fields were only grey with scattered snow,
And now the longest grass-leaves hardly emerge;
Yet her deep footsteps mark the snow, and go
On towards the pines at the hills' white verge.

I cannot see her, since the mist's white scarf
Obscures the dark wood and the dull orange sky;
But she's waiting, I know, impatient and cold, half
Sobs struggling into her frosty sigh.

Why does she come so promptly, when she must know
That she's only the nearer to the inevitable farewell;
The hill is steep, on the snow my steps are slow—
Why does she come, when she knows what I have to tell?

EPILOGUE

Patience, little Heart.
One day a heavy, June-hot woman
Will enter and shut the door to stay.

And when your stifling heart would summon
Cool, lonely night, her roused breasts will keep the night at bay,
Sitting in your room like two tiger-lilies
Flaming on after sunset,
Destroying the cool, lonely night with the glow of their hot twilight;
There in the morning, still, while the fierce strange scent comes yet
Stronger, hot and red; till you thirst for the daffodillies
With an anguished, husky thirst that you cannot assuage,
When the daffodillies are dead, and a woman of the dog-days holds you
        in gage.
Patience, little Heart.

A BABY RUNNING BAREFOOT

When the bare feet of the baby beat across the grass
The little white feet nod like white flowers in the wind,
They poise and run like ripples lapping across the water;
And the sight of their white play among the grass
Is like a little robin's song, winsome,
Or as two white butterflies settle in the cup of one flower
For a moment, then away with a flutter of wings.

I long for the baby to wander hither to me
Like a wind-shadow wandering over the water,
So that she can stand on my knee
With her little bare feet in my hands,
Cool like syringa buds,
Firm and silken like pink young peony flowers.

DISCIPLINE

It is stormy, and raindrops cling like silver bees to the pane,
The thin sycamores in the playground are swinging with flattened
        leaves;
The heads of the boys move dimly through a yellow gloom that stains
The class; over them all the dark net of my discipline weaves.

It is no good, dear, gentleness and forbearance, I endured too long.
I have pushed my hands in the dark soil, under the flower of my soul
And the gentle leaves, and have felt where the roots are strong
Fixed in the darkness, grappling for the deep soil's little control.

And there is the dark, my darling, where the roots are entangled and
        fight
Each one for its hold on the oblivious darkness, I know that there
In the night where we first have being, before we rise on the light,
We are not brothers, my darling, we fight and we do not spare.

And in the original dark the roots cannot keep, cannot know
Any communion whatever, but they bind themselves on to the dark,
And drawing the darkness together, crush from it a twilight, a slow
Burning that breaks at last into leaves and a flower's bright spark.

I came to the boys with love, my dear, but they turned on me;
I came with gentleness, with my heart 'twixt my hands like a bowl,
Like a loving-cup, like a grail, but they spilt it triumphantly
And tried to break the vessel, and to violate my soul.

But what have I to do with the boys, deep down in my soul, my love?
I throw from out of the darkness my self like a flower into sight,
Like a flower from out of the night-time, I lift my face, and those
Who will may warm their hands at me, comfort this night.

But whosoever would pluck apart my flowering shall burn their hands,
So flowers are tender folk, and roots can only hide,
Yet my flowerings of love are a fire, and the scarlet brands
Of my love are roses to look at, but flames to chide.

But comfort me, my love, now the fires are low,
Now I am broken to earth like a winter destroyed, and all
Myself but a knowledge of roots, of roots in the dark that throw
A net on the undersoil, which lies passive beneath their thrall.

But comfort me, for henceforth my love is yours alone,
To you alone will I offer the bowl, to you will I give
My essence only, but love me, and I will atone
To you for my general loving, atone as long as I live.

SCENT OF IRISES

A faint, sickening scent of irises
Persists all morning. Here in a jar on the table
A fine proud spike of purple irises
Rising above the class-room litter, makes me unable
To see the class's lifted and bended faces
Save in a broken pattern, amid purple and gold and sable.

I can smell the gorgeous bog-end, in its breathless
Dazzle of may-blobs, when the marigold glare overcast you
With fire on your cheeks and your brow and your chin as you dipped
Your face in the marigold bunch, to touch and contrast you,
Your own dark mouth with the bridal faint lady-smocks,
Dissolved on the golden sorcery you should not outlast.

You amid the bog-end's yellow incantation,
You sitting in the cowslips of the meadow above,
Me, your shadow on the bog-flame, flowery may-blobs,
Me full length in the cowslips, muttering you love;
You, your soul like a lady-smock, lost, evanescent,
You with your face all rich, like the sheen of a dove.

You are always asking, do I remember, remember
The butter-cup bog-end where the flowers rose up
And kindled you over deep with a cast of gold?
You ask again, do the healing days close up
The open darkness which then drew us in,
The dark which then drank up our brimming cup.

You upon the dry, dead beech-leaves, in the fire of night
Burnt like a sacrifice; you invisible;
Only the fire of darkness, and the scent of you!
—And yes, thank God, it still is possible
The healing days shall close the darkness up
Wherein we fainted like a smoke or dew.

Like vapour, dew, or poison. Now, thank God,
The fire of night is gone, and your face is ash
Indistinguishable on the grey, chill day;
The night has burnt us out, at last the good
Dark fire burns on untroubled, without clash
Of you upon the dead leaves saying me Yea.

THE PROPHET

Ah, my darling, when over the purple horizon shall loom
The shrouded mother of a new idea, men hide their faces,
Cry out and fend her off, as she seeks her procreant groom,
Wounding themselves against her, denying her fecund embraces.

LAST WORDS TO MIRIAM

Yours is the shame and sorrow
    But the disgrace is mine;
Your love was dark and thorough,
Mine was the love of the sun for a flower
    He creates with his shine.

I was diligent to explore you,
    Blossom you stalk by stalk,
Till my fire of creation bore you
Shrivelling down in the final dour
    Anguish—then I suffered a balk.

I knew your pain, and it broke
    My fine, craftsman's nerve;
Your body quailed at my stroke,
And my courage failed to give you the last
    Fine torture you did deserve.

You are shapely, you are adorned,
   But opaque and dull in the flesh,
Who, had I but pierced with the thorned
Fire-threshing anguish, were fused and cast
   In a lovely illumined mesh.

Like a painted window: the best
   Suffering burnt through your flesh,
Undrossed it and left it blest
With a quivering sweet wisdom of grace: but now
   Who shall take you afresh?

Now who will burn you free
   From your body's terrors and dross,
Since the fire has failed in me?
What man will stoop in your flesh to plough
   The shrieking cross?

A mute, nearly beautiful thing
   Is your face, that fills me with shame
As I see it hardening,
Warping the perfect image of God,
   And darkening my eternal fame.

MYSTERY

Now I am all
One bowl of kisses,
Such as the tall
Slim votaresses
Of Egypt filled
For a God's excesses.

I lift to you
My bowl of kisses,
And through the temple's
Blue recesses
Cry out to you
In wild caresses.

And to my lips'
Bright crimson rim
The passion slips,
And down my slim
White body drips
The shining hymn.

And still before
The altar I
Exult the bowl
Brimful, and cry
To you to stoop
And drink, Most High.

Oh drink me up
That I may be
Within your cup
Like a mystery,
Like wine that is still
In ecstasy.

Glimmering still
In ecstasy,
Commingled wines
Of you and me
In one fulfil
The mystery.

PATIENCE

A Wind comes from the north
Blowing little flocks of birds
Like spray across the town,
And a train, roaring forth,
Rushes stampeding down
With cries and flying curds
Of steam, out of the darkening north.

Whither I turn and set
Like a needle steadfastly,
Waiting ever to get
The news that she is free;
But ever fixed, as yet,
To the lode of her agony.

BALLAD OF ANOTHER OPHELIA

Oh the green glimmer of apples in the orchard,
Lamps in a wash of rain!
Oh the wet walk of my brown hen through the stack-yard,
Oh tears on the window pane!

Nothing now will ripen the bright green apples,
Full of disappointment and of rain,
Brackish they will taste, of tears, when the yellow dapples
Of autumn tell the withered tale again.

All round the yard it is cluck, my brown hen,
Cluck, and the rain-wet wings,
Cluck, my marigold bird, and again
Cluck for your yellow darlings.

For the grey rat found the gold thirteen
Huddled away in the dark,
Flutter for a moment, oh the beast is quick and keen,
Extinct one yellow-fluffy spark.

Once I had a lover bright like running water,
Once his face was laughing like the sky;
Open like the sky looking down in all its laughter
On the buttercups, and the buttercups was I.

What, then, is there hidden in the skirts of all the blossom?
What is peeping from your wings, oh mother hen?
'Tis the sun who asks the question, in a lovely haste for wisdom;
What a lovely haste for wisdom is in men!

Yea, but it is cruel when undressed is all the blossom,
And her shift is lying white upon the floor,
That a grey one, like a shadow, like a rat, a thief, a rain-storm,
Creeps upon her then and gathers in his store.

Oh the grey garner that is full of half-grown apples,
Oh the golden sparkles laid extinct!
And oh, behind the cloud-sheaves, like yellow autumn dapples,
Did you see the wicked sun that winked!

RESTLESSNESS

At the open door of the room I stand and look at the night,
Hold my hand to catch the raindrops, that slant into sight,
Arriving grey from the darkness above suddenly into the light of the
    room.
I will escape from the hollow room, the box of light,
And be out in the bewildering darkness, which is always fecund, which
        might
Mate my hungry soul with a germ of its womb.

I will go out to the night, as a man goes down to the shore
To draw his net through the surfs thin line, at the dawn before
The sun warms the sea, little, lonely and sad, sifting the sobbing tide.
I will sift the surf that edges the night, with my net, the four
Strands of my eyes and my lips and my hands and my feet, sifting the
        store
Of flotsam until my soul is tired or satisfied.

I will catch in my eyes' quick net
The faces of all the women as they go past,
Bend over them with my soul, to cherish the wet
Cheeks and wet hair a moment, saying: "Is it you?"
Looking earnestly under the dark umbrellas, held fast
Against the wind; and if, where the lamplight blew
Its rainy swill about us, she answered me
With a laugh and a merry wildness that it was she
Who was seeking me, and had found me at last to free
Me now from the stunting bonds of my chastity,
How glad I should be!

Moving along in the mysterious ebb of the night
Pass the men whose eyes are shut like anemones in a dark pool;
Why don't they open with vision and speak to me, what have they in
        sight?
Why do I wander aimless among them, desirous fool?

I can always linger over the huddled books on the stalls,
Always gladden my amorous fingers with the touch of their leaves,
Always kneel in courtship to the shelves in the doorways, where falls
The shadow, always offer myself to one mistress, who always receives.

But oh, it is not enough, it is all no good.
There is something I want to feel in my running blood,
Something I want to touch; I must hold my face to the rain,
I must hold my face to the wind, and let it explain
Me its life as it hurries in secret.
I will trail my hands again through the drenched, cold leaves
Till my hands are full of the chillness and touch of leaves,
Till at length they induce me to sleep, and to forget.

A BABY ASLEEP AFTER PAIN

As a drenched, drowned bee
Hangs numb and heavy from a bending flower,
   So clings to me
My baby, her brown hair brushed with wet tears
   And laid against her cheek;
Her soft white legs hanging heavily over my arm
Swinging heavily to my movement as I walk.
   My sleeping baby hangs upon my life,
Like a burden she hangs on me.
   She has always seemed so light,
But now she is wet with tears and numb with pain
Even her floating hair sinks heavily,
   Reaching downwards;
As the wings of a drenched, drowned bee
   Are a heaviness, and a weariness.

ANXIETY

The hoar-frost crumbles in the sun,
   The crisping steam of a train
Melts in the air, while two black birds
   Sweep past the window again.

Along the vacant road, a red
   Bicycle approaches; I wait
In a thaw of anxiety, for the boy
   To leap down at our gate.

He has passed us by; but is it
   Relief that starts in my breast?
Or a deeper bruise of knowing that still
   She has no rest.

THE PUNISHER

I have fetched the tears up out of the little wells,
Scooped them up with small, iron words,
   Dripping over the runnels.

The harsh, cold wind of my words drove on, and still
I watched the tears on the guilty cheek of the boys
   Glitter and spill.

Cringing Pity, and Love, white-handed, came
Hovering about the Judgment which stood in my eyes,
    Whirling a flame.

   . . . .

The tears are dry, and the cheeks' young fruits are fresh
With laughter, and clear the exonerated eyes, since pain
    Beat through the flesh.

The Angel of Judgment has departed again to the Nearness.
Desolate I am as a church whose lights are put out.
    And night enters in drearness.

The fire rose up in the bush and blazed apace,
The thorn-leaves crackled and twisted and sweated in anguish;
    Then God left the place.

Like a flower that the frost has hugged and let go, my head
Is heavy, and my heart beats slowly, laboriously,
    My strength is shed.

THE END

If I could have put you in my heart,
If but I could have wrapped you in myself,
How glad I should have been!
And now the chart
Of memory unrolls again to me
The course of our journey here, before we had to part.

And oh, that you had never, never been
Some of your selves, my love, that some
Of your several faces I had never seen!
And still they come before me, and they go,
And I cry aloud in the moments that intervene.

And oh, my love, as I rock for you to-night,
And have not any longer any hope
To heal the suffering, or make requite
For all your life of asking and despair,
I own that some of me is dead to-night.

64

THE BRIDE

My love looks like a girl to-night,
        But she is old.
The plaits that lie along her pillow
        Are not gold,
But threaded with filigree,
        And uncanny cold.

She looks like a young maiden, since her brow
        Is smooth and fair,
Her cheeks are very smooth, her eyes are closed,
        She sleeps a rare
Still winsome sleep, so still, and so composed.

Nay, but she sleeps like a bride, and dreams her dreams
        Of perfect things.
She lies at last, the darling, in the shape of her dream,
        And her dead mouth sings
By its shape, like the thrushes in clear evenings.

THE VIRGIN MOTHER

My little love, my darling,
You were a doorway to me;
You let me out of the confines
Into this strange countrie,
Where people are crowded like thistles,
Yet are shapely and comely to see.

My little love, my dearest
Twice have you issued me,
Once from your womb, sweet mother,
Once from myself, to be
Free of all hearts, my darling,
Of each heart's home-life free.

And so, my love, my mother,
I shall always be true to you;
Twice I am born, my dearest,
To life, and to death, in you;
And this is the life hereafter
Wherein I am true.

I kiss you good-bye, my darling,
Our ways are different now;
You are a seed in the night-time,
I am a man, to plough
The difficult glebe of the future
For God to endow.

I kiss you good-bye, my dearest,
It is finished between us here.
Oh, if I were calm as you are,
Sweet and still on your bier!
God, if I had not to leave you
Alone, my dear!

Let the last word be uttered,
Oh grant the farewell is said!
Spare me the strength to leave you
Now you are dead.
I must go, but my soul lies helpless
Beside your bed.

AT THE WINDOW

The pine-trees bend to listen to the autumn wind as it mutters
Something which sets the black poplars ashake with hysterical laughter;
While slowly the house of day is closing its eastern shutters.

Further down the valley the clustered tombstones recede,
Winding about their dimness the mist's grey cerements, after
The street lamps in the darkness have suddenly started to bleed.

The leaves fly over the window and utter a word as they pass
To the face that leans from the darkness, intent, with two dark-filled
        eyes
That watch for ever earnestly from behind the window glass.

DRUNK

Too far away, oh love, I know,
To save me from this haunted road,
Whose lofty roses break and blow
On a night-sky bent with a load

Of lights: each solitary rose,
Each arc-lamp golden does expose
Ghost beyond ghost of a blossom, shows
Night blenched with a thousand snows.

Of hawthorn and of lilac trees,
White lilac; shows discoloured night
Dripping with all the golden lees
Laburnum gives back to light

And shows the red of hawthorn set
On high to the purple heaven of night,
Like flags in blenched blood newly wet,
Blood shed in the noiseless fight.

Of life for love and love for life,
Of hunger for a little food,
Of kissing, lost for want of a wife
Long ago, long ago wooed.

.   .   .   .   .   .

Too far away you are, my love,
To steady my brain in this phantom show
That passes the nightly road above
And returns again below.

The enormous cliff of horse-chestnut trees
    Has poised on each of its ledges
An erect small girl looking down at me;
White-night-gowned little chits I see,
    And they peep at me over the edges
Of the leaves as though they would leap, should I call
    Them down to my arms;
"But, child, you're too small for me, too small
    Your little charms."

White little sheaves of night-gowned maids,
    Some other will thresh you out!
And I see leaning from the shades
A lilac like a lady there, who braids
    Her white mantilla about
Her face, and forward leans to catch the sight
    Of a man's face,
Gracefully sighing through the white
    Flowery mantilla of lace.

And another lilac in purple veiled
    Discreetly, all recklessly calls
In a low, shocking perfume, to know who has hailed
    Her forth from the night: my strength has failed
In her voice, my weak heart falls:
Oh, and see the laburnum shimmering
      Her draperies down,
As if she would slip the gold, and glimmering
    White, stand naked of gown.

         .   .   .   .   .   .

The pageant of flowery trees above
    The street pale-passionate goes,
And back again down the pavement, Love
    In a lesser pageant flows.

Two and two are the folk that walk,
    They pass in a half embrace
Of linkèd bodies, and they talk
    With dark face leaning to face.

Come then, my love, come as you will
    Along this haunted road,
Be whom you will, my darling, I shall
    Keep with you the troth I trowed.

SORROW

Why does the thin grey strand
Floating up from the forgotten
Cigarette between my fingers,
Why does it trouble me?

Ah, you will understand;
When I carried my mother downstairs,
A few times only, at the beginning
Of her soft-foot malady,

I should find, for a reprimand
To my gaiety, a few long grey hairs
On the breast of my coat; and one by one
I let them float up the dark chimney.

DOLOR OF AUTUMN

The acrid scents of autumn,
Reminiscent of slinking beasts, make me fear
Everything, tear-trembling stars of autumn
And the snore of the night in my ear.

For suddenly, flush-fallen,
All my life, in a rush
Of shedding away, has left me
Naked, exposed on the bush.

I, on the bush of the globe,
Like a newly-naked berry, shrink
Disclosed: but I also am prowling
As well in the scents that slink

Abroad: I in this naked berry
Of flesh that stands dismayed on the bush;
And I in the stealthy, brindled odours
Prowling about the lush

And acrid night of autumn;
My soul, along with the rout,
Rank and treacherous, prowling,
Disseminated out.

For the night, with a great breath intaken,
Has taken my spirit outside
Me, till I reel with disseminated consciousness,
Like a man who has died.

At the same time I stand exposed
Here on the bush of the globe,
A newly-naked berry of flesh
For the stars to probe.

THE INHERITANCE

Since you did depart
Out of my reach, my darling,
Into the hidden,
I see each shadow start
With recognition, and I
Am wonder-ridden.

I am dazed with the farewell,
But I scarcely feel your loss.
You left me a gift
Of tongues, so the shadows tell
Me things, and silences toss
Me their drift.

You sent me a cloven fire
Out of death, and it burns in the draught
Of the breathing hosts,
Kindles the darkening pyre
For the sorrowful, till strange brands waft
Like candid ghosts.

Form after form, in the streets
Waves like a ghost along,
Kindled to me;
The star above the house-top greets
Me every eve with a long
Song fierily.

All day long, the town
Glimmers with subtle ghosts
Going up and down
In a common, prison-like dress;
But their daunted looking flickers
To me, and I answer, Yes!

So I am not lonely nor sad
Although bereaved of you,
My little love.
I move among a kinsfolk clad
With words, but the dream shows through
As they move.

SILENCE

Since I lost you I am silence-haunted,
  Sounds wave their little wings
A moment, then in weariness settle
  On the flood that soundless swings.

Whether the people in the street
  Like pattering ripples go by,
Or whether the theatre sighs and sighs
  With a loud, hoarse sigh:

Or the wind shakes a ravel of light
  Over the dead-black river,
Or night's last echoing
  Makes the daybreak shiver:

I feel the silence waiting
  To take them all up again
In its vast completeness, enfolding
  The sound of men.

LISTENING

I listen to the stillness of you,
  My dear, among it all;
I feel your silence touch my words as I talk,
  And take them in thrall.

My words fly off a forge
  The length of a spark;
I see the night-sky easily sip them
  Up in the dark.

The lark sings loud and glad,
  Yet I am not loth
That silence should take the song and the bird
  And lose them both.

A train goes roaring south,
  The steam-flag flying;
I see the stealthy shadow of silence
  Alongside going.

And off the forge of the world,
  Whirling in the draught of life,
Go sparks of myriad people, filling
  The night with strife.

Yet they never change the darkness
  Or blench it with noise;
Alone on the perfect silence
  The stars are buoys.

BROODING GRIEF

A yellow leaf from the darkness
Hops like a frog before me.
Why should I start and stand still?

I was watching the woman that bore me
Stretched in the brindled darkness
Of the sick-room, rigid with will
To die: and the quick leaf tore me
Back to this rainy swill
Of leaves and lamps and traffic mingled before me.

LOTUS HURT BY THE COLD

How many times, like lotus lilies risen
   Upon the surface of a river, there
   Have risen floating on my blood the rare
Soft glimmers of my hope escaped from prison.

So I am clothed all over with the light
   And sensitive beautiful blossoming of passion;
   Till naked for her in the finest fashion
The flowers of all my mud swim into sight.

And then I offer all myself unto
   This woman who likes to love me: but she turns
   A look of hate upon the flower that burns
To break and pour her out its precious dew.

And slowly all the blossom shuts in pain,
   And all the lotus buds of love sink over
   To die unopened: when my moon-faced lover,
Kind on the weight of suffering, smiles again.

MALADE

The sick grapes on the chair by the bed lie prone; at the window
The tassel of the blind swings gently, tapping the pane,
As a little wind comes in.
The room is the hollow rind of a fruit, a gourd
Scooped out and dry, where a spider,
Folded in its legs as in a bed,
Lies on the dust, watching where is nothing to see but twilight and
      walls.

And if the day outside were mine! What is the day
But a grey cave, with great grey spider-cloths hanging
Low from the roof, and the wet dust falling softly from them
Over the wet dark rocks, the houses, and over
The spiders with white faces, that scuttle on the floor of the cave!
I am choking with creeping, grey confinedness.

But somewhere birds, beside a lake of light, spread wings
Larger than the largest fans, and rise in a stream upwards
And upwards on the sunlight that rains invisible,
So that the birds are like one wafted feather,
Small and ecstatic suspended over a vast spread country.

LIAISON

A big bud of moon hangs out of the twilight,
   Star-spiders spinning their thread
Hang high suspended, withouten respite
   Watching us overhead.

Come then under the trees, where the leaf-cloths
   Curtain us in so dark
That here we're safe from even the ermin-moth's
   Flitting remark.

Here in this swarthy, secret tent,
   Where black boughs flap the ground,
You shall draw the thorn from my discontent,
   Surgeon me sound.

This rare, rich night! For in here
   Under the yew-tree tent
The darkness is loveliest where I could sear
   You like frankincense into scent.

Here not even the stars can spy us,
   Not even the white moths write
With their little pale signs on the wall, to try us
   And set us affright.

Kiss but then the dust from off my lips,
   But draw the turgid pain
From my breast to your bosom, eclipse
   My soul again.

Waste me not, I beg you, waste
   Not the inner night:
Taste, oh taste and let me taste
   The core of delight.

TROTH WITH THE DEAD

The moon is broken in twain, and half a moon
Before me lies on the still, pale floor of the sky;
The other half of the broken coin of troth
Is buried away in the dark, where the still dead lie.
They buried her half in the grave when they laid her away;
I had pushed it gently in among the thick of her hair
Where it gathered towards the plait, on that very last day;
And like a moon in secret it is shining there.

My half shines in the sky, for a general sign
Of the troth with the dead I pledged myself to keep;
Turning its broken edge to the dark, it shines indeed
Like the sign of a lover who turns to the dark of sleep.
Against my heart the inviolate sleep breaks still
In darkened waves whose breaking echoes o'er
The wondering world of my wakeful day, till I'm lost
In the midst of the places I knew so well before.

DISSOLUTE

Many years have I still to burn, detained
Like a candle flame on this body; but I enshrine
A darkness within me, a presence which sleeps contained
In my flame of living, her soul enfolded in mine.

And through these years, while I burn on the fuel of life,
What matter the stuff I lick up in my living flame,
Seeing I keep in the fire-core, inviolate,
A night where she dreams my dreams for me, ever the same.

SUBMERGENCE

When along the pavement,
Palpitating flames of life,
People flicker round me,
I forget my bereavement,
The gap in the great constellation,
The place where a star used to be.

Nay, though the pole-star
Is blown out like a candle,
And all the heavens are wandering in disarray,
Yet when pleiads of people are
Deployed around me, and I see
The street's long outstretched Milky Way,

When people flicker down the pavement,
I forget my bereavement.

THE ENKINDLED SPRING

This spring as it comes bursts up in bonfires green,
Wild puffing of emerald trees, and flame-filled bushes,
Thorn-blossom lifting in wreaths of smoke between
Where the wood fumes up and the watery, flickering rushes.

I am amazed at this spring, this conflagration
Of green fires lit on the soil of the earth, this blaze
Of growing, and sparks that puff in wild gyration,
Faces of people streaming across my gaze.

And I, what fountain of fire am I among
This leaping combustion of spring? My spirit is tossed
About like a shadow buffeted in the throng
Of flames, a shadow that's gone astray, and is lost.

REPROACH

Had I but known yesterday,
Helen, you could discharge the ache
    Out of the cloud;
Had I known yesterday you could take
The turgid electric ache away,
    Drink it up with your proud
White body, as lovely white lightning
Is drunk from an agonised sky by the earth,
I might have hated you, Helen.

But since my limbs gushed full of fire,
Since from out of my blood and bone
    Poured a heavy flame
To you, earth of my atmosphere, stone
Of my steel, lovely white flint of desire,
    You have no name.
Earth of my swaying atmosphere,
Substance of my inconstant breath,
I cannot but cleave to you.

Since you have drunken up the drear
Painful electric storm, and death
    Is washed from the blue
Of my eyes, I see you beautiful.
You are strong and passive and beautiful,
I come like winds that uncertain hover;
    But you
Are the earth I hover over.

THE HANDS OF THE BETROTHED

Her tawny eyes are onyx of thoughtlessness,
Hardened they are like gems in ancient modesty;
Yea, and her mouth's prudent and crude caress
Means even less than her many words to me.

Though her kiss betrays me also this, this only
Consolation, that in her lips her blood at climax clips
Two wild, dumb paws in anguish on the lonely
Fruit of my heart, ere down, rebuked, it slips.

I know from her hardened lips that still her heart is
Hungry for me, yet if I put my hand in her breast
She puts me away, like a saleswoman whose mart is
Endangered by the pilferer on his quest.

But her hands are still the woman, the large, strong hands
Heavier than mine, yet like leverets caught in steel
When I hold them; my still soul understands
Their dumb confession of what her sort must feel.

For never her hands come nigh me but they lift
Like heavy birds from the morning stubble, to settle
Upon me like sleeping birds, like birds that shift
Uneasily in their sleep, disturbing my mettle.

How caressingly she lays her hand on my knee,
How strangely she tries to disown it, as it sinks
In my flesh and bone and forages into me,
How it stirs like a subtle stoat, whatever she thinks!

And often I see her clench her fingers tight
And thrust her fists suppressed in the folds of her skirt;
And sometimes, how she grasps her arms with her bright
Big hands, as if surely her arms did hurt.

And I have seen her stand all unaware
Pressing her spread hands over her breasts, as she
Would crush their mounds on her heart, to kill in there
The pain that is her simple ache for me.

Her strong hands take my part, the part of a man
To her; she crushes them into her bosom deep
Where I should lie, and with her own strong span
Closes her arms, that should fold me in sleep.

Ah, and she puts her hands upon the wall,
Presses them there, and kisses her bright hands,
Then lets her black hair loose, the darkness fall
About her from her maiden-folded bands.

And sits in her own dark night of her bitter hair
Dreaming—God knows of what, for to me she's the same
Betrothed young lady who loves me, and takes care
Of her womanly virtue and of my good name.

EXCURSION

I wonder, can the night go by;
Can this shot arrow of travel fly
Shaft-golden with light, sheer into the sky
    Of a dawned to-morrow,
Without ever sleep delivering us
From each other, or loosing the dolorous
    Unfruitful sorrow!

What is it then that you can see
That at the window endlessly
You watch the red sparks whirl and flee
    And the night look through?
Your presence peering lonelily there
Oppresses me so, I can hardly bear
    To share the train with you.

You hurt my heart-beats' privacy;
I wish I could put you away from me;
I suffocate in this intimacy,
    For all that I love you;
How I have longed for this night in the train,
Yet now every fibre of me cries in pain
    To God to remove you.

But surely my soul's best dream is still
That one night pouring down shall swill
Us away in an utter sleep, until
    We are one, smooth-rounded.
Yet closely bitten in to me
Is this armour of stiff reluctancy
    That keeps me impounded.

So, dear love, when another night
Pours on us, lift your fingers white
And strip me naked, touch me light,
    Light, light all over.
For I ache most earnestly for your touch,
Yet I cannot move, however much
    I would be your lover.

Night after night with a blemish of day
Unblown and unblossomed has withered away;
Come another night, come a new night, say
    Will you pluck me apart?
Will you open the amorous, aching bud
Of my body, and loose the burning flood
    That would leap to you from my heart?

PERFIDY

Hollow rang the house when I knocked on the door,
And I lingered on the threshold with my hand
Upraised to knock and knock once more:
Listening for the sound of her feet across the floor,
Hollow re-echoed my heart.

The low-hung lamps stretched down the road
With shadows drifting underneath,
With a music of soft, melodious feet
Quickening my hope as I hastened to meet
The low-hung light of her eyes.

The golden lamps down the street went out,
The last car trailed the night behind;
And I in the darkness wandered about
With a flutter of hope and of dark-shut doubt
In the dying lamp of my love.

Two brown ponies trotting slowly
Stopped at a dim-lit trough to drink:
The dark van drummed down the distance slowly;
While the city stars so dim and holy
Drew nearer to search through the streets.

A hastening car swept shameful past,
I saw her hid in the shadow,
I saw her step to the curb, and fast
Run to the silent door, where last
I had stood with my hand uplifted.
She clung to the door in her haste to enter,
Entered, and quickly cast
It shut behind her, leaving the street aghast.

A SPIRITUAL WOMAN

Close your eyes, my love, let me make you blind;
     They have taught you to see
Only a mean arithmetic on the face of things,
A cunning algebra in the faces of men,
     And God like geometry
Completing his circles, and working cleverly.

I'll kiss you over the eyes till I kiss you blind;
     If I can—if any one could.
Then perhaps in the dark you'll have got what you want to find.
You've discovered so many bits, with your clever eyes,
     And I'm a kaleidoscope
That you shake and shake, and yet it won't come to your mind.
Now stop carping at me.—But God, how I hate you!
     Do you fear I shall swindle you?
Do you think if you take me as I am, that that will abate you
Somehow?—so sad, so intrinsic, so spiritual, yet so cautious, you
Must have me all in your will and your consciousness—
     I hate you.

MATING

Round clouds roll in the arms of the wind,
The round earth rolls in a clasp of blue sky,
And see, where the budding hazels are thinned,
    The wild anemones lie
In undulating shivers beneath the wind.

Over the blue of the waters ply
White ducks, a living flotilla of cloud;
And, look you, floating just thereby,
    The blue-gleamed drake stems proud
Like Abraham, whose seed should multiply.

In the lustrous gleam of the water, there
Scramble seven toads across the silk, obscure leaves,
Seven toads that meet in the dusk to share
    The darkness that interweaves
The sky and earth and water and live things everywhere.

Look now, through the woods where the beech-green spurts
Like a storm of emerald snow, look, see
  A great bay stallion dances, skirts
    The bushes sumptuously,
Going outward now in the spring to his brief deserts.

Ah love, with your rich, warm face aglow,
What sudden expectation opens you
  So wide as you watch the catkins blow
    Their dust from the birch on the blue
Lift of the pulsing wind—ah, tell me you know!

Ah, surely! Ah, sure from the golden sun
A quickening, masculine gleam floats in to all
  Us creatures, people and flowers undone,
    Lying open under his thrall,
As he begets the year in us. What, then, would you shun?

Why, I should think that from the earth there fly
Fine thrills to the neighbour stars, fine yellow beams
  Thrown lustily off from our full-blown, high
    Bursting globe of dreams,
To quicken the spheres that are virgin still in the sky.

Do you not hear each morsel thrill
With joy at travelling to plant itself within
  The expectant one, therein to instil
    New rapture, new shape to win,
From the thick of life wake up another will?

Surely, and if that I would spill
The vivid, ah, the fiery surplus of life,
  From off my brimming measure, to fill
    You, and flush you rife
With increase, do you call it evil, and always evil?

A LOVE SONG

Reject me not if I should say to you
I do forget the sounding of your voice,
I do forget your eyes that searching through
The mists perceive our marriage, and rejoice.

Yet, when the apple-blossom opens wide
Under the pallid moonlight's fingering,
I see your blanched face at my breast, and hide
My eyes from diligent work, malingering.

Ah, then, upon my bedroom I do draw
The blind to hide the garden, where the moon
Enjoys the open blossoms as they straw
Their beauty for his taking, boon for boon.

And I do lift my aching arms to you,
And I do lift my anguished, avid breast,
And I do weep for very pain of you,
And fling myself at the doors of sleep, for rest.

And I do toss through the troubled night for you,
Dreaming your yielded mouth is given to mine,
Feeling your strong breast carry me on into
The peace where sleep is stronger even than wine.

BROTHER AND SISTER

The shorn moon trembling indistinct on her path,
Frail as a scar upon the pale blue sky,
Draws towards the downward slope; some sorrow hath
Worn her down to the quick, so she faintly fares
Along her foot-searched way without knowing why
She creeps persistent down the sky's long stairs.

Some say they see, though I have never seen,
The dead moon heaped within the new moon's arms;
For surely the fragile, fine young thing had been
Too heavily burdened to mount the heavens so.
But my heart stands still, as a new, strong dread alarms
Me; might a young girl be heaped with such shadow of woe?

Since Death from the mother moon has pared us down to the quick,
And cast us forth like shorn, thin moons, to travel
An uncharted way among the myriad thick
Strewn stars of silent people, and luminous litter
Of lives which sorrows like mischievous dark mice chavel
To nought, diminishing each star's glitter,

Since Death has delivered us utterly, naked and white,
Since the month of childhood is over, and we stand alone,
Since the beloved, faded moon that set us alight
Is delivered from us and pays no heed though we moan
In sorrow, since we stand in bewilderment, strange
And fearful to sally forth down the sky's long range.

We may not cry to her still to sustain us here,
We may not hold her shadow back from the dark.
Oh, let us here forget, let us take the sheer
Unknown that lies before us, bearing the ark
Of the covenant onwards where she cannot go.
Let us rise and leave her now, she will never know.

AFTER MANY DAYS

I wonder if with you, as it is with me,
If under your slipping words, that easily flow
About you as a garment, easily,
    Your violent heart beats to and fro!

Long have I waited, never once confessed,
Even to myself, how bitter the separation;
Now, being come again, how make the best
    Reparation?

If I could cast this clothing off from me,
If I could lift my naked self to you,
Or if only you would repulse me, a wound would be
    Good; it would let the ache come through.

But that you hold me still so kindly cold
Aloof my flaming heart will not allow;
Yea, but I loathe you that you should withhold
    Your pleasure now.

BLUE

The earth again like a ship steams out of the dark sea over
The edge of the blue, and the sun stands up to see us glide
Slowly into another day; slowly the rover
Vessel of darkness takes the rising tide.

I, on the deck, am startled by this dawn confronting
Me who am issued amazed from the darkness, stripped
And quailing here in the sunshine, delivered from haunting
The night unsounded whereon our days are shipped.

Feeling myself undawning, the day's light playing upon me,
I who am substance of shadow, I all compact
Of the stuff of the night, finding myself all wrongly
Among the crowds of things in the sunshine jostled and racked.

I with the night on my lips, I sigh with the silence of death;
And what do I care though the very stones should cry me unreal,
        though the clouds
Shine in conceit of substance upon me, who am less than the rain.
Do I not know the darkness within them? What are they but shrouds?

The clouds go down the sky with a wealthy ease
Casting a shadow of scorn upon me for my share in death; but I
Hold my own in the midst of them, darkling, defy
The whole of the day to extinguish the shadow I lift on the breeze.

Yea, though the very clouds have vantage over me,
Enjoying their glancing flight, though my love is dead,
I still am not homeless here, I've a tent by day
Of darkness where she sleeps on her perfect bed.

And I know the host, the minute sparkling of darkness
Which vibrates untouched and virile through the grandeur of night,
But which, when dawn crows challenge, assaulting the vivid motes
Of living darkness, bursts fretfully, and is bright:

  Runs like a fretted arc-lamp into light,
  Stirred by conflict to shining, which else
  Were dark and whole with the night.

  Runs to a fret of speed like a racing wheel,
  Which else were aslumber along with the whole
  Of the dark, swinging rhythmic instead of a-reel.

Is chafed to anger, bursts into rage like thunder;
Which else were a silent grasp that held the heavens
Arrested, beating thick with wonder.

Leaps like a fountain of blue sparks leaping
In a jet from out of obscurity,
Which erst was darkness sleeping.

Runs into streams of bright blue drops,
Water and stones and stars, and myriads
Of twin-blue eyes, and crops

Of floury grain, and all the hosts of day,
All lovely hosts of ripples caused by fretting
The Darkness into play.

SNAP-DRAGON

She bade me follow to her garden, where
The mellow sunlight stood as in a cup
Between the old grey walls; I did not dare
To raise my face, I did not dare look up,
Lest her bright eyes like sparrows should fly in
My windows of discovery, and shrill "Sin."

So with a downcast mien and laughing voice
I followed, followed the swing of her white dress
That rocked in a lilt along: I watched the poise
Of her feet as they flew for a space, then paused to press
The grass deep down with the royal burden of her:
And gladly I'd offered my breast to the tread of her.

"I like to see," she said, and she crouched her down,
She sunk into my sight like a settling bird;
And her bosom couched in the confines of her gown
Like heavy birds at rest there, softly stirred
By her measured breaths: "I like to see," said she,
"The snap-dragon put out his tongue at me."

She laughed, she reached her hand out to the flower,
Closing its crimson throat. My own throat in her power
Strangled, my heart swelled up so full
As if it would burst its wine-skin in my throat,
Choke me in my own crimson. I watched her pull
The gorge of the gaping flower, till the blood did float

Over my eyes, and I was blind—
Her large brown hand stretched over
The windows of my mind;
And there in the dark I did discover
Things I was out to find:
My Grail, a brown bowl twined
With swollen veins that met in the wrist,
Under whose brown the amethyst
I longed to taste. I longed to turn
My heart's red measure in her cup,
I longed to feel my hot blood burn
With the amethyst in her cup.

Then suddenly she looked up,
And I was blind in a tawny-gold day,
Till she took her eyes away.
So she came down from above
And emptied my heart of love.
So I held my heart aloft
To the cuckoo that hung like a dove,
And she settled soft

It seemed that I and the morning world
Were pressed cup-shape to take this reiver
Bird who was weary to have furled
Her wings in us,
As we were weary to receive her.

This bird, this rich,
Sumptuous central grain,
This mutable witch,
This one refrain,
This laugh in the fight,
This clot of night,
This core of delight.

She spoke, and I closed my eyes
To shut hallucinations out.
I echoed with surprise
Hearing my mere lips shout
The answer they did devise.

Again I saw a brown bird hover
Over the flowers at my feet;
I felt a brown bird hover
Over my heart, and sweet
Its shadow lay on my heart.

I thought I saw on the clover
A brown bee pulling apart
The closed flesh of the clover
And burrowing in its heart.

She moved her hand, and again
I felt the brown bird cover
My heart; and then
The bird came down on my heart,
As on a nest the rover
Cuckoo comes, and shoves over
The brim each careful part
Of love, takes possession, and settles her down,
With her wings and her feathers to drown
The nest in a heat of love.

She turned her flushed face to me for the glint
Of a moment. "See," she laughed, "if you also
Can make them yawn." I put my hand to the dint
In the flower's throat, and the flower gaped wide with woe.
She watched, she went of a sudden intensely still,
She watched my hand, to see what I would fulfil.

I pressed the wretched, throttled flower between
My fingers, till its head lay back, its fangs
Poised at her. Like a weapon my hand was white and keen,
And I held the choked flower-serpent in its pangs
Of mordant anguish, till she ceased to laugh,
Until her pride's flag, smitten, cleaved down to the staff.

She hid her face, she murmured between her lips
The low word "Don't." I let the flower fall,
But held my hand afloat towards the slips
Of blossom she fingered, and my fingers all
Put forth to her: she did not move, nor I,
For my hand like a snake watched hers, that could not fly.

Then I laughed in the dark of my heart, I did exult
Like a sudden chuckling of music. I bade her eyes
Meet mine, I opened her helpless eyes to consult
Their fear, their shame, their joy that underlies
Defeat in such a battle. In the dark of her eyes
My heart was fierce to make her laughter rise.

Till her dark deeps shook with convulsive thrills, and the dark
Of her spirit wavered like water thrilled with light;
And my heart leaped up in longing to plunge its stark
Fervour within the pool of her twilight,
Within her spacious soul, to grope in delight.

And I do not care, though the large hands of revenge
Shall get my throat at last, shall get it soon,
If the joy that they are searching to avenge
Have risen red on my night as a harvest moon,
Which even death can only put out for me;
And death, I know, is better than not-to-be.

A PASSING BELL

Mournfully to and fro, to and fro the trees are waving;
        What did you say, my dear?
The rain-bruised leaves are suddenly shaken, as a child
Asleep still shakes in the clutch of a sob—
        Yes, my love, I hear.

One lonely bell, one only, the storm-tossed afternoon is braving,
        Why not let it ring?
The roses lean down when they hear it, the tender, mild
Flowers of the bleeding-heart fall to the throb—
        It is such a little thing!

A wet bird walks on the lawn, call to the boy to come and look,
        Yes, it is over now.
Call to him out of the silence, call him to see
The starling shaking its head as it walks in the grass—
        Ah, who knows how?

He cannot see it, I can never show it him, how it shook—
        Don't disturb him, darling.
—Its head as it walked: I can never call him to me,
Never, he is not, whatever shall come to pass.
        No, look at the wet starling.

IN TROUBLE AND SHAME

    I look at the swaling sunset
    And wish I could go also
Through the red doors beyond the black-purple bar.

I wish that I could go
Through the red doors where I could put off
   My shame like shoes in the porch,
   My pain like garments,
And leave my flesh discarded lying
Like luggage of some departed traveller
   Gone one knows not where.

   Then I would turn round,
And seeing my cast-off body lying like lumber,
   I would laugh with joy.

ELEGY

Since I lost you, my darling, the sky has come near,
And I am of it, the small sharp stars are quite near,
The white moon going among them like a white bird among snow-
     berries,
And the sound of her gently rustling in heaven like a bird I hear.

And I am willing to come to you now, my dear,
As a pigeon lets itself off from a cathedral dome
To be lost in the haze of the sky, I would like to come,
And be lost out of sight with you, and be gone like foam.

For I am tired, my dear, and if I could lift my feet,
My tenacious feet from off the dome of the earth
To fall like a breath within the breathing wind
Where you are lost, what rest, my love, what rest!

GREY EVENING

When you went, how was it you carried with you
My missal book of fine, flamboyant hours?
My book of turrets and of red-thorn bowers,
And skies of gold, and ladies in bright tissue?

Now underneath a blue-grey twilight, heaped
Beyond the withering snow of the shorn fields
Stands rubble of stunted houses; all is reaped
And garnered that the golden daylight yields.

Dim lamps like yellow poppies glimmer among
The shadowy stubble of the under-dusk,
As farther off the scythe of night is swung,
And little stars come rolling from their husk.

And all the earth is gone into a dust
Of greyness mingled with a fume of gold,
Covered with aged lichens, pale with must,
And all the sky has withered and gone cold.

And so I sit and scan the book of grey,
Feeling the shadows like a blind man reading,
All fearful lest I find the last words bleeding
With wounds of sunset and the dying day.

FIRELIGHT AND NIGHTFALL

The darkness steals the forms of all the queens,
But oh, the palms of his two black hands are red,
Inflamed with binding up the sheaves of dead
Hours that were once all glory and all queens.

And I remember all the sunny hours
Of queens in hyacinth and skies of gold,
And morning singing where the woods are scrolled
And diapered above the chaunting flowers.

Here lamps are white like snowdrops in the grass;
The town is like a churchyard, all so still
And grey now night is here; nor will
Another torn red sunset come to pass.

THE MYSTIC BLUE

Out of the darkness, fretted sometimes in its sleeping,
Jets of sparks in fountains of blue come leaping
To sight, revealing a secret, numberless secrets keeping.

Sometimes the darkness trapped within a wheel
Runs into speed like a dream, the blue of the steel
Showing the rocking darkness now a-reel.

And out of the invisible, streams of bright blue drops
Rain from the showery heavens, and bright blue crops
Surge from the under-dark to their ladder-tops.

And all the manifold blue and joyous eyes,
The rainbow arching over in the skies,
New sparks of wonder opening in surprise.

All these pure things come foam and spray of the sea
Of Darkness abundant, which shaken mysteriously,
Breaks into dazzle of living, as dolphins that leap from the sea
Of midnight shake it to fire, so the secret of death we see.

LOOK! WE HAVE COME THROUGH! (1917)

Some of these poems have appeared in the "English Review" and in "Poetry," also in the "Georgian Anthology" and the "Imagist Anthology"

FOREWORD

These poems should not be considered separately, as so many single pieces. They are intended as an essential story, or history, or confession, unfolding one from the other in organic development, the whole revealing the intrinsic experience of a man during the crisis of manhood, when he marries and comes into himself. The period covered is, roughly, the sixth lustre of a man's life

ARGUMENT

*After much struggling and loss in love and in
the world of man, the protagonist throws in
his lot with a woman who is already married.
Together they go into another country, she
perforce leaving her children behind. The
conflict of love and hate goes on between the
man and the woman, and between these two
and the world around them, till it reaches
some sort of conclusion, they transcend into
some condition of blessedness*

MOONRISE

And who has seen the moon, who has not seen
Her rise from out the chamber of the deep,
Flushed and grand and naked, as from the chamber
Of finished bridegroom, seen her rise and throw
Confession of delight upon the wave,
Littering the waves with her own superscription
Of bliss, till all her lambent beauty shakes towards us
Spread out and known at last, and we are sure
That beauty is a thing beyond the grave,
That perfect, bright experience never falls
To nothingness, and time will dim the moon
Sooner than our full consummation here
In this odd life will tarnish or pass away.

ELEGY

The sun immense and rosy
Must have sunk and become extinct
The night you closed your eyes for ever against me.

Grey days, and wan, dree dawnings
Since then, with fritter of flowers—
Day wearies me with its ostentation and fawnings.

Still, you left me the nights,
The great dark glittery window,
The bubble hemming this empty existence with lights.

Still in the vast hollow
Like a breath in a bubble spinning
Brushing the stars, goes my soul, that skims the bounds like a swallow!

I can look through
The film of the bubble night, to where you are.
Through the film I can almost touch you.

EASTWOOD

NONENTITY

The stars that open and shut
Fall on my shallow breast
Like stars on a pool.

The soft wind, blowing cool
Laps little crest after crest
Of ripples across my breast.

And dark grass under my feet
Seems to dabble in me
Like grass in a brook.

Oh, and it is sweet
To be all these things, not to be
Any more myself.

For look,
I am weary of myself!

MARTYR À LA MODE

Ah God, life, law, so many names you keep,
You great, you patient Effort, and you Sleep
That does inform this various dream of living,
You sleep stretched out for ever, ever giving
Us out as dreams, you august Sleep
Coursed round by rhythmic movement of all time,

The constellations, your great heart, the sun
Fierily pulsing, unable to refrain;
Since you, vast, outstretched, wordless Sleep
Permit of no beyond, ah you, whose dreams
We are, and body of sleep, let it never be said
I quailed at my appointed function, turned poltroon

For when at night, from out the full surcharge
Of a day's experience, sleep does slowly draw
The harvest, the spent action to itself;
Leaves me unburdened to begin again;
At night, I say, when I am gone in sleep,
Does my slow heart rebel, do my dead hands
Complain of what the day has had them do?

Never let it be said I was poltroon
At this my task of living, this my dream,
This me which rises from the dark of sleep
In white flesh robed to drape another dream,
As lightning comes all white and trembling
From out the cloud of sleep, looks round about
One moment, sees, and swift its dream is over,
In one rich drip it sinks to another sleep,
And sleep thereby is one more dream enrichened.

If so the Vast, the God, the Sleep that still grows richer
Have said that I, this mote in the body of sleep
Must in my transiency pass all through pain,
Must be a dream of grief, must like a crude
Dull meteorite flash only into light
When tearing through the anguish of this life,
Still in full flight extinct, shall I then turn
Poltroon, and beg the silent, outspread God
To alter my one speck of doom, when round me burns
The whole great conflagration of all life,
Lapped like a body close upon a sleep,
Hiding and covering in the eternal Sleep
Within the immense and toilsome life-time, heaved

With ache of dreams that body forth the Sleep?

Shall I, less than the least red grain of flesh
Within my body, cry out to the dreaming soul
That slowly labours in a vast travail,
To halt the heart, divert the streaming flow
That carries moons along, and spare the stress
That crushes me to an unseen atom of fire?

When pain and all
And grief are but the same last wonder, Sleep
Rising to dream in me a small keen dream
Of sudden anguish, sudden over and spent—

CROYDON

DON JUAN

It is Isis the mystery
Must be in love with me.

Here this round ball of earth
Where all the mountains sit
Solemn in groups,
And the bright rivers flit
Round them for girth.

Here the trees and troops
Darken the shining grass,
And many people pass
Plundered from heaven,
Many bright people pass,
Plunder from heaven.

What of the mistresses
What the beloved seven?
—They were but witnesses,
I was just driven.

Where is there peace for me?
Isis the mystery
Must be in love with me.

THE SEA

You, you are all unloving, loveless, you;
Restless and lonely, shaken by your own moods,
You are celibate and single, scorning a comrade even,
Threshing your own passions with no woman for the threshing-floor,
Finishing your dreams for your own sake only,
Playing your great game around the world, alone,
Without playmate, or helpmate, having no one to cherish,
No one to comfort, and refusing any comforter.

Not like the earth, the spouse all full of increase
Moiled over with the rearing of her many-mouthed young;
You are single, you are fruitless, phosphorescent, cold and callous,
Naked of worship, of love or of adornment,
Scorning the panacea even of labour,
Sworn to a high and splendid purposelessness
Of brooding and delighting in the secret of life's goings,
Sea, only you are free, sophisticated.

You who toil not, you who spin not,
Surely but for you and your like, toiling
Were not worth while, nor spinning worth the effort!

You who take the moon as in a sieve, and sift
Her flake by flake and spread her meaning out;
You who roll the stars like jewels in your palm,
So that they seem to utter themselves aloud;
You who steep from out the days their colour,
Reveal the universal tint that dyes
Their web; who shadow the sun's great gestures and expressions
So that he seems a stranger in his passing;
Who voice the dumb night fittingly;
Sea, you shadow of all things, now mock us to death with your
        shadowing.

BOURNEMOUTH

HYMN TO PRIAPUS

My love lies underground
With her face upturned to mine,
And her mouth unclosed in a last long kiss
That ended her life and mine.

I dance at the Christmas party
Under the mistletoe
Along with a ripe, slack country lass
Jostling to and fro.

The big, soft country lass,
Like a loose sheaf of wheat
Slipped through my arms on the threshing floor
At my feet.

The warm, soft country lass,
Sweet as an armful of wheat
At threshing-time broken, was broken
For me, and ah, it was sweet!

Now I am going home
Fulfilled and alone,
I see the great Orion standing
Looking down.

He's the star of my first beloved
Love-making.
The witness of all that bitter-sweet
Heart-aching.

Now he sees this as well,
This last commission.
Nor do I get any look
Of admonition.

He can add the reckoning up
I suppose, between now and then,
Having walked himself in the thorny, difficult
Ways of men.

He has done as I have done
No doubt:
Remembered and forgotten
Turn and about.

My love lies underground
With her face upturned to mine,
And her mouth unclosed in the last long kiss
That ended her life and mine.

She fares in the stark immortal
Fields of death;
I in these goodly, frozen
Fields beneath.

Something in me remembers
And will not forget.
The stream of my life in the darkness
Deathward set!

And something in me has forgotten,
Has ceased to care.
Desire comes up, and contentment
Is debonair.

I, who am worn and careful,
How much do I care?
How is it I grin then, and chuckle
Over despair?

Grief, grief, I suppose and sufficient
Grief makes us free
To be faithless and faithful together
As we have to be.

BALLAD OF A WILFUL WOMAN

FIRST PART

Upon her plodding palfrey
With a heavy child at her breast
And Joseph holding the bridle
They mount to the last hill-crest.

Dissatisfied and weary
She sees the blade of the sea
Dividing earth and heaven
In a glitter of ecstasy.

Sudden a dark-faced stranger
With his back to the sun, holds out
His arms; so she lights from her palfrey
And turns her round about.

98

She has given the child to Joseph,
Gone down to the flashing shore;
And Joseph, shading his eyes with his hand,
Stands watching evermore.

SECOND PART

The sea in the stones is singing,
A woman binds her hair
With yellow, frail sea-poppies,
That shine as her fingers stir.

While a naked man comes swiftly
Like a spurt of white foam rent
From the crest of a falling breaker,
Over the poppies sent.

He puts his surf-wet fingers
Over her startled eyes,
And asks if she sees the land, the land,
The land of her glad surmise.

THIRD PART

Again in her blue, blue mantle
Riding at Joseph's side,
She says, "I went to Cythera,
And woe betide!"

Her heart is a swinging cradle
That holds the perfect child,
But the shade on her forehead ill becomes
A mother mild.

So on with the slow, mean journey
In the pride of humility;
Till they halt at a cliff on the edge of the land
Over a sullen sea.

While Joseph pitches the sleep-tent
She goes far down to the shore
To where a man in a heaving boat
Waits with a lifted oar.

FOURTH PART

They dwelt in a huge, hoarse sea-cave
And looked far down the dark
Where an archway torn and glittering
Shone like a huge sea-spark.

He said: "Do you see the spirits
Crowding the bright doorway?"
He said: "Do you hear them whispering?"
He said: "Do you catch what they say?"

FIFTH PART

Then Joseph, grey with waiting,
His dark eyes full of pain,
Heard: "I have been to Patmos;
Give me the child again."

Now on with the hopeless journey
Looking bleak ahead she rode,
And the man and the child of no more account
Than the earth the palfrey trode.

Till a beggar spoke to Joseph,
But looked into her eyes;
So she turned, and said to her husband:
"I give, whoever denies."

SIXTH PART

She gave on the open heather
Beneath bare judgment stars,
And she dreamed of her children and Joseph,
And the isles, and her men, and her scars.

And she woke to distil the berries
The beggar had gathered at night,
Whence he drew the curious liquors
He held in delight.

He gave her no crown of flowers,
No child and no palfrey slow,
Only led her through harsh, hard places
Where strange winds blow.

She follows his restless wanderings
Till night when, by the fire's red stain,
Her face is bent in the bitter steam
That comes from the flowers of pain.

Then merciless and ruthless
He takes the flame-wild drops
To the town, and tries to sell them
With the market-crops.

So she follows the cruel journey
That ends not anywhere,
And dreams, as she stirs the mixing-pot,
She is brewing hope from despair.

TRIER

FIRST MORNING

THE night was a failure
    but why not—?

In the darkness
    with the pale dawn seething at the window
    through the black frame
    I could not be free,
    not free myself from the past, those others—
    and our love was a confusion,
    there was a horror,
    you recoiled away from me.

Now, in the morning
As we sit in the sunshine on the seat by the little shrine,
And look at the mountain-walls,
Walls of blue shadow,
And see so near at our feet in the meadow
Myriads of dandelion pappus
Bubbles ravelled in the dark green grass
Held still beneath the sunshine—

It is enough, you are near—
The mountains are balanced,
The dandelion seeds stay half-submerged in the grass;
You and I together
We hold them proud and blithe
On our love.
They stand upright on our love,
Everything starts from us,
We are the source.

BEUERBERG

"AND OH—THAT THE MAN I AM MIGHT CEASE TO BE—"

No, now I wish the sunshine would stop,
and the white shining houses, and the gay red flowers on the balconies
and the bluish mountains beyond, would be crushed out
between two valves of darkness;
the darkness falling, the darkness rising, with muffled sound
obliterating everything.

I wish that whatever props up the walls of light
would fall, and darkness would come hurling heavily down,
and it would be thick black dark for ever.
Not sleep, which is grey with dreams,
nor death, which quivers with birth,
but heavy, sealing darkness, silence, all immovable.

What is sleep?
It goes over me, like a shadow over a hill,
but it does not alter me, nor help me.
And death would ache still, I am sure;
it would be lambent, uneasy.
I wish it would be completely dark everywhere,
inside me, and out, heavily dark
utterly.

WOLFRATSHAUSEN

SHE LOOKS BACK

The pale bubbles
The lovely pale-gold bubbles of the globe-flowers
In a great swarm clotted and single
Went rolling in the dusk towards the river
To where the sunset hung its wan gold cloths;
And you stood alone, watching them go,
And that mother-love like a demon drew you from me
Towards England.

Along the road, after nightfall,
Along the glamorous birch-tree avenue
Across the river levels
We went in silence, and you staring to England.

So then there shone within the jungle darkness
Of the long, lush under-grass, a glow-worm's sudden
Green lantern of pure light, a little, intense, fusing triumph,
White and haloed with fire-mist, down in the tangled darkness.

Then you put your hand in mine again, kissed me, and we struggled to
        be together.
And the little electric flashes went with us, in the grass,
Tiny lighthouses, little souls of lanterns, courage burst into an
        explosion of green light
Everywhere down in the grass, where darkness was ravelled in
        darkness.

Still, the kiss was a touch of bitterness on my mouth
Like salt, burning in.
And my hand withered in your hand.
For you were straining with a wild heart, back, back again,
Back to those children you had left behind, to all the æons of the past.
And I was here in the under-dusk of the Isar.

At home, we leaned in the bedroom window
Of the old Bavarian Gasthaus,
And the frogs in the pool beyond thrilled with exuberance,
Like a boiling pot the pond crackled with happiness,
Like a rattle a child spins round for joy, the night rattled
With the extravagance of the frogs,
And you leaned your cheek on mine,
And I suffered it, wanting to sympathise.

At last, as you stood, your white gown falling from your breasts,
You looked into my eyes, and said: "But this is joy!"
I acquiesced again.
But the shadow of lying was in your eyes,
The mother in you, fierce as a murderess, glaring to England,
Yearning towards England, towards your young children,
Insisting upon your motherhood, devastating.

Still, the joy was there also, you spoke truly,
The joy was not to be driven off so easily;
Stronger than fear or destructive mother-love, it stood flickering;
The frogs helped also, whirring away.
Yet how I have learned to know that look in your eyes
Of horrid sorrow!
How I know that glitter of salt, dry, sterile, sharp, corrosive salt!
Not tears, but white sharp brine
Making hideous your eyes.

I have seen it, felt it in my mouth, my throat, my chest, my belly,
Burning of powerful salt, burning, eating through my defenceless
        nakedness.
I have been thrust into white, sharp crystals,
Writhing, twisting, superpenetrated.

Ah, Lot's Wife, Lot's Wife!
The pillar of salt, the whirling, horrible column of salt, like a
        waterspout
That has enveloped me!
Snow of salt, white, burning, eating salt
In which I have writhed.

Lot's Wife!—Not Wife, but Mother.
I have learned to curse your motherhood,
You pillar of salt accursed.
I have cursed motherhood because of you,
Accursed, base motherhood!

I long for the time to come, when the curse against you will have gone
        out of my heart.
But it has not gone yet.
Nevertheless, once, the frogs, the globe-flowers of
Bavaria, the glow-worms
Gave me sweet lymph against the salt-burns,
There is a kindness in the very rain.

Therefore, even in the hour of my deepest, passionate malediction
I try to remember it is also well between us.
That you are with me in the end.
That you never look quite back; nine-tenths, ah, more
You look round over your shoulder;
But never quite back.

Nevertheless the curse against you is still in my heart
Like a deep, deep burn.
The curse against all mothers.
All mothers who fortify themselves in motherhood, devastating the
        vision.
They are accursed, and the curse is not taken off
It burns within me like a deep, old burn,
And oh, I wish it was better.

     BEUERBERG

ON THE BALCONY

In front of the sombre mountains, a faint, lost ribbon of rainbow;
And between us and it, the thunder;
And down below in the green wheat, the labourers
Stand like dark stumps, still in the green wheat.

You are near to me, and your naked feet in their sandals,
And through the scent of the balcony's naked timber
I distinguish the scent of your hair: so now the limber
Lightning falls from heaven.

Adown the pale-green glacier river floats
A dark boat through the gloom—and whither?
The thunder roars. But still we have each other!
The naked lightnings in the heavens dither
And disappear—what have we but each other?
The boat has gone.

     ICKING

FROHNLEICHNAM

You have come your way, I have come my way;
You have stepped across your people, carelessly, hurting them all;
I have stepped across my people, and hurt them in spite of my care.

But steadily, surely, and notwithstanding
We have come our ways and met at last
Here in this upper room.

Here the balcony
Overhangs the street where the bullock-wagons slowly
Go by with their loads of green and silver birch-trees
For the feast of Corpus Christi.

Here from the balcony
We look over the growing wheat, where the jade-green river
Goes between the pine-woods,
Over and beyond to where the many mountains
Stand in their blueness, flashing with snow and the morning.

I have done; a quiver of exultation goes through me, like the first
Breeze of the morning through a narrow white birch.
You glow at last like the mountain tops when they catch
Day and make magic in heaven.

At last I can throw away world without end, and meet you
Unsheathed and naked and narrow and white;
At last you can throw immortality off, and I see you
Glistening with all the moment and all your beauty.

Shameless and callous I love you;
Out of indifference I love you;
Out of mockery we dance together,
Out of the sunshine into the shadow,
Passing across the shadow into the sunlight,
Out of sunlight to shadow.

As we dance
Your eyes take all of me in as a communication;
As we dance
I see you, ah, in full!
Only to dance together in triumph of being together
Two white ones, sharp, vindicated,
Shining and touching,
Is heaven of our own, sheer with repudiation.

IN THE DARK

A blotch of pallor stirs beneath the high
Square picture-dusk, the window of dark sky.

A sound subdued in the darkness: tears!
As if a bird in difficulty up the valley steers.

"Why have you gone to the window? Why don't you sleep?
How you have wakened me! But why, why do you weep?"

"*I am afraid of you, I am afraid, afraid!*
There is something in you destroys me—!"

"You have dreamed and are not awake, come here to me."
"*No, I have wakened. It is you, you are cruel to me!*"

"My dear!"—"*Yes, yes, you are cruel to me. You cast*
A shadow over my breasts that will kill me at last."

"Come!"—"*No, I'm a thing of life. I give*
You armfuls of sunshine, and you won't let me live."

"Nay, I'm too sleepy!"—"*Ah, you are horrible;*
You stand before me like ghosts, like a darkness upright."

"I!"—"*How can you treat me so, and love me?*
My feet have no hold, you take the sky from above me."

"My dear, the night is soft and eternal, no doubt
You love it!"—"*It is dark, it kills me, I am put out.*"

"My dear, when you cross the street in the sun-shine, surely
Your own small night goes with you. Why treat it so poorly?"

"*No, no, I dance in the sun, I'm a thing of life—*"
"Even then it is dark behind you. Turn round, my wife."

"*No, how cruel you are, you people the sunshine*
With shadows!"—"With yours I people the sunshine, yours and mine—"

"In the darkness we all are gone, we are gone with the trees
And the restless river;—we are lost and gone with all these."

"*But I am myself, I have nothing to do with these.*"
"Come back to bed, let us sleep on our mysteries.

"Come to me here, and lay your body by mine,
And I will be all the shadow, you the shine.

"Come, you are cold, the night has frightened you.
Hark at the river! It pants as it hurries through

"The pine-woods. How I love them so, in their mystery of not-to-be."
"—*But let me be myself, not a river or a tree.*"

"Kiss me! How cold you are!—Your little breasts
Are bubbles of ice. Kiss me!—You know how it rests

"One to be quenched, to be given up, to be gone in the dark;
To be blown out, to let night dowse the spark.

"But never mind, my love. Nothing matters, save sleep;
Save you, and me, and sleep; all the rest will keep."

MUTILATION

A thick mist-sheet lies over the broken wheat.
I walk up to my neck in mist, holding my mouth up.
Across there, a discoloured moon burns itself out.

I hold the night in horror;
I dare not turn round.

To-night I have left her alone.
They would have it I have left her for ever.

Oh my God, how it aches
Where she is cut off from me!

Perhaps she will go back to England.
Perhaps she will go back,
Perhaps we are parted for ever.

If I go on walking through the whole breadth of Germany
I come to the North Sea, or the Baltic.

Over there is Russia—Austria, Switzerland, France, in a circle!
I here in the undermist on the Bavarian road.

It aches in me.
What is England or France, far off,
But a name she might take?
I don't mind this continent stretching, the sea far away;
It aches in me for her
Like the agony of limbs cut off and aching;
Not even longing,
It is only agony.

A cripple!
Oh God, to be mutilated!
To be a cripple!

And if I never see her again?

I think, if they told me so
I could convulse the heavens with my horror.
I think I could alter the frame of things in my agony.
I think I could break the System with my heart.
I think, in my convulsion, the skies would break.

She too suffers.
But who could compel her, if she chose me against them all?
She has not chosen me finally, she suspends her choice.
Night folk, Tuatha De Danaan, dark Gods, govern her sleep,
Magnificent ghosts of the darkness, carry off her decision in sleep,
Leave her no choice, make her lapse me-ward, make her,
Oh Gods of the living Darkness, powers of Night.

WOLFRATSHAUSEN

HUMILIATION

I have been so innerly proud, and so long alone,
Do not leave me, or I shall break.
Do not leave me.

What should I do if you were gone again
So soon?
What should I look for?
Where should I go?
What should I be, I myself,
"I"?
What would it mean, this
I?

Do not leave me.

What should I think of death?
If I died, it would not be you:
It would be simply the same
Lack of you.
The same want, life or death,
Unfulfilment,
The same insanity of space
You not there for me.

Think, I daren't die
For fear of the lack in death.
And I daren't live.

Unless there were a morphine or a drug.

I would bear the pain.
But always, strong, unremitting
It would make me not me.
The thing with my body that would go on living
Would not be me.
Neither life nor death could help.

Think, I couldn't look towards death
Nor towards the future:
Only not look.
Only myself
Stand still and bind and blind myself.

God, that I have no choice!
That my own fulfilment is up against me
Timelessly!
The burden of self-accomplishment!
The charge of fulfilment!
And God, that she is *necessary!*
Necessary, and I have no choice!

Do not leave me.

A YOUNG WIFE

The pain of loving you
Is almost more than I can bear.

I walk in fear of you.
The darkness starts up where
You stand, and the night comes through
Your eyes when you look at me.

Ah never before did I see
The shadows that live in the sun!

Now every tall glad tree
Turns round its back to the sun
And looks down on the ground, to see
The shadow it used to shun.

At the foot of each glowing thing
A night lies looking up.

Oh, and I want to sing
And dance, but I can't lift up
My eyes from the shadows: dark
They lie spilt round the cup.

What is it?—Hark
The faint fine seethe in the air!

Like the seething sound in a shell!
It is death still seething where
The wild-flower shakes its bell
And the sky lark twinkles blue—

The pain of loving you
Is almost more than I can bear.

GREEN

The dawn was apple-green,
  The sky was green wine held up in the sun,
The moon was a golden petal between.

She opened her eyes, and green
  They shone, clear like flowers undone
For the first time, now for the first time seen.

ICKING

RIVER ROSES

By the Isar, in the twilight
We were wandering and singing,
By the Isar, in the evening
We climbed the huntsman's ladder and sat swinging
In the fir-tree overlooking the marshes,
While river met with river, and the ringing
Of their pale-green glacier water filled the evening.

By the Isar, in the twilight
We found the dark wild roses
Hanging red at the river; and simmering
Frogs were singing, and over the river closes
Was savour of ice and of roses; and glimmering
Fear was abroad. We whispered: "No one knows us.
Let it be as the snake disposes
Here in this simmering marsh."

KLOSTER SCHAEFTLARN

GLOIRE DE DIJON

When she rises in the morning
I linger to watch her;
She spreads the bath-cloth underneath the window
And the sunbeams catch her
Glistening white on the shoulders,
While down her sides the mellow
Golden shadow glows as
She stoops to the sponge, and her swung breasts
Sway like full-blown yellow
Gloire de Dijon roses.

She drips herself with water, and her shoulders
Glisten as silver, they crumple up
Like wet and falling roses, and I listen
For the sluicing of their rain-dishevelled petals.
In the window full of sunlight
Concentrates her golden shadow
Fold on fold, until it glows as
Mellow as the glory roses.

ICKING

ROSES ON THE BREAKFAST TABLE

Just a few of the roses we gathered from the Isar
Are fallen, and their mauve-red petals on the cloth
Float like boats on a river, while other
Roses are ready to fall, reluctant and loth.

She laughs at me across the table, saying
I am beautiful. I look at the rumpled young roses
And suddenly realise, in them as in me,
How lovely the present is that this day discloses.

I AM LIKE A ROSE

I AM myself at last; now I achieve
My very self. I, with the wonder mellow,
Full of fine warmth, I issue forth in clear
And single me, perfected from my fellow.

Here I am all myself. No rose-bush heaving
Its limpid sap to culmination, has brought
Itself more sheer and naked out of the green
In stark-clear roses, than I to myself am brought.

ROSE OF ALL THE WORLD

I am here myself; as though this heave of effort
At starting other life, fulfilled my own:
Rose-leaves that whirl in colour round a core
Of seed-specks kindled lately and softly blown

By all the blood of the rose-bush into being—
Strange, that the urgent will in me, to set
My mouth on hers in kisses, and so softly
To bring together two strange sparks, beget

Another life from our lives, so should send
The innermost fire of my own dim soul out-spinning
And whirling in blossom of flame and being upon me!
That my completion of manhood should be the beginning

Another life from mine! For so it looks.
The seed is purpose, blossom accident.
The seed is all in all, the blossom lent
To crown the triumph of this new descent.

Is that it, woman? Does it strike you so?
The Great Breath blowing a tiny seed of fire
Fans out your petals for excess of flame,
Till all your being smokes with fine desire?

Or are we kindled, you and I, to be
One rose of wonderment upon the tree
Of perfect life, and is our possible seed
But the residuum of the ecstasy?

How will you have it?—the rose is all in all,
Or the ripe rose-fruits of the luscious fall?
The sharp begetting, or the child begot?
Our consummation matters, or does it not?

To me it seems the seed is just left over
From the red rose-flowers' fiery transience;
Just orts and slarts; berries that smoulder in the bush
Which burnt just now with marvellous immanence.

Blossom, my darling, blossom, be a rose
Of roses unchidden and purposeless; a rose
For rosiness only, without an ulterior motive;
For me it is more than enough if the flower unclose.

A YOUTH MOWING

There are four men mowing down by the Isar;
I can hear the swish of the scythe-strokes, four
Sharp breaths taken: yea, and I
Am sorry for what's in store.

The first man out of the four that's mowing
Is mine, I claim him once and for all;
Though it's sorry I am, on his young feet, knowing
None of the trouble he's led to stall.

As he sees me bringing the dinner, he lifts
His head as proud as a deer that looks
Shoulder-deep out of the corn; and wipes
His scythe-blade bright, unhooks

The scythe-stone and over the stubble to me.
Lad, thou hast gotten a child in me,
Laddie, a man thou'lt ha'e to be,
Yea, though I'm sorry for thee.

QUITE FORSAKEN

What pain, to wake and miss you!
   To wake with a tightened heart,
And mouth reaching forward to kiss you!

This then at last is the dawn, and the bell
   Clanging at the farm! Such bewilderment
Comes with the sight of the room, I cannot tell.

It is raining. Down the half-obscure road
   Four labourers pass with their scythes
Dejectedly;—a huntsman goes by with his load:

A gun, and a bunched-up deer, its four little feet
   Clustered dead.—And this is the dawn
For which I wanted the night to retreat!

FORSAKEN AND FORLORN

The house is silent, it is late at night, I am alone.
        From the balcony
     I can hear the Isar moan,
       Can see the white
Rift of the river eerily, between the pines, under a sky of stone.

Some fireflies drift through the middle air
       Tinily.
     I wonder where
Ends this darkness that annihilates me.

FIREFLIES IN THE CORN

She speaks.
Look at the little darlings in the corn!
   The rye is taller than you, who think yourself
So high and mighty: look how the heads are borne
   Dark and proud on the sky, like a number of knights
Passing with spears and pennants and manly scorn.

Knights indeed!—much knight I know will ride
   With his head held high-serene against the sky!
Limping and following rather at my side
   Moaning for me to love him!—Oh darling rye
How I adore you for your simple pride!

And the dear, dear fireflies wafting in between
   And over the swaying corn-stalks, just above
All the dark-feathered helmets, like little green
   Stars come low and wandering here for love
Of these dark knights, shedding their delicate sheen!

I thank you I do, you happy creatures, you dears
   Riding the air, and carrying all the time
Your little lanterns behind you! Ah, it cheers
   My soul to see you settling and trying to climb
The corn-stalks, tipping with fire the spears.

All over the dim corn's motion, against the blue
  Dark sky of night, a wandering glitter, a swarm
Of questing brilliant souls going out with their true
  Proud knights to battle! Sweet, how I warm
My poor, my perished soul with the sight of you!

A DOE AT EVENING

As I went through the marshes
a doe sprang out of the corn
and flashed up the hill-side
leaving her fawn.

On the sky-line
she moved round to watch,
she pricked a fine black blotch
on the sky.

I looked at her
and felt her watching;
I became a strange being.
Still, I had my right to be there with her,

Her nimble shadow trotting
along the sky-line, she
put back her fine, level-balanced head.
And I knew her.

Ah yes, being male, is not my head hard-balanced, antlered?
Are not my haunches light?
Has she not fled on the same wind with me?
Does not my fear cover her fear?

IRSCHENHAUSEN

SONG OF A MAN WHO IS NOT LOVED

The space of the world is immense, before me and around me;
If I turn quickly, I am terrified, feeling space surround me;
Like a man in a boat on very clear, deep water, space frightens and
      confounds me.

I see myself isolated in the universe, and wonder
What effect I can have. My hands wave under
The heavens like specks of dust that are floating asunder.

I hold myself up, and feel a big wind blowing
Me like a gadfly into the dusk, without my knowing
Whither or why or even how I am going.

So much there is outside me, so infinitely
Small am I, what matter if minutely
I beat my way, to be lost immediately?

How shall I flatter myself that I can do
Anything in such immensity? I am too
Little to count in the wind that drifts me through.

GLASHÜTTE

SINNERS

The big mountains sit still in the afternoon light
    Shadows in their lap;
The bees roll round in the wild-thyme with delight.

We sitting here among the cranberries
    So still in the gap
Of rock, distilling our memories

Are sinners! Strange! The bee that blunders
    Against me goes off with a laugh.
A squirrel cocks his head on the fence, and wonders

What about sin?—For, it seems
    The mountains have
No shadow of us on their snowy forehead of dreams

As they ought to have. They rise above us
    Dreaming
For ever. One even might think that they love us.

   Little red cranberries cheek to cheek,
   Two great dragon-flies wrestling;
   You, with your forehead nestling
   Against me, and bright peak shining to peak—

There's a love-song for you!—Ah, if only
    There were no teeming
Swarms of mankind in the world, and we were less lonely!

MAYRHOFEN

MISERY

Out of this oubliette between the mountains
five valleys go, five passes like gates;
three of them black in shadow, two of them bright
with distant sunshine;
and sunshine fills one high valley bed,
green grass shining, and little white houses
like quartz crystals,
little, but distinct a way off.

Why don't I go?
Why do I crawl about this pot, this oubliette,
stupidly?
Why don't I go?

But where?
If I come to a pine-wood, I can't say
Now I am arrived!
What are so many straight trees to me!

STERZING

SUNDAY AFTERNOON IN ITALY

The man and the maid go side by side
With an interval of space between;
And his hands are awkward and want to hide,
She braves it out since she must be seen.

When some one passes he drops his head
Shading his face in his black felt hat,
While the hard girl hardens; nothing is said,
There is nothing to wonder or cavil at.

Alone on the open road again
With the mountain snows across the lake
Flushing the afternoon, they are uncomfortable,
The loneliness daunts them, their stiff throats ache.

And he sighs with relief when she parts from him;
Her proud head held in its black silk scarf
Gone under the archway, home, he can join
The men that lounge in a group on the wharf.

118

His evening is a flame of wine
Among the eager, cordial men.
And she with her women hot and hard
Moves at her ease again.

She is marked, she is singled out
    For the fire:
The brand is upon him, look—you,
    Of desire.

They are chosen, ah, they are fated
    For the fight!
Champion her, all you women! Men, menfolk
    Hold him your light!

Nourish her, train her, harden her
    Women all!
Fold him, be good to him, cherish him
    Men, ere he fall.

Women, another champion!
    This, men, is yours!
Wreathe and enlap and anoint them
    Behind separate doors.

GARGNANO

WINTER DAWN

Green star Sirius
Dribbling over the lake;
The stars have gone so far on their road,
Yet we're awake!

Without a sound
The new young year comes in
And is half-way over the lake.
We must begin

Again. This love so full
Of hate has hurt us so,
We lie side by side
Moored—but no,

Let me get up
And wash quite clean
Of this hate.—
So green

The great star goes!
I am washed quite clean,
Quite clean of it all.
But e'en

So cold, so cold and clean
Now the hate is gone!
It is all no good,
I am chilled to the bone

Now the hate is gone;
There is nothing left;
I am pure like bone,
Of all feeling bereft.

A BAD BEGINNING

The yellow sun steps over the mountain-top
And falters a few short steps across the lake—
Are you awake?

See, glittering on the milk-blue, morning lake
They are laying the golden racing-track of the sun;
The day has begun.

The sun is in my eyes, I must get up.
I want to go, there's a gold road blazes before
My breast—which is so sore.

What?—your throat is bruised, bruised with my kisses?
Ah, but if I am cruel what then are you?
I am bruised right through.

What if I love you!—This misery
Of your dissatisfaction and misprision
Stupefies me.

Ah yes, your open arms! Ah yes, ah yes,
You would take me to your breast!—But no,
You should come to mine,
It were better so.

Here I am—get up and come to me!
Not as a visitor either, nor a sweet
And winsome child of innocence; nor
As an insolent mistress telling my pulse's beat.

Come to me like a woman coming home
To the man who is her husband, all the rest
Subordinate to this, that he and she
Are joined together for ever, as is best.

Behind me on the lake I hear the steamer drumming
From Austria. There lies the world, and here
Am I. Which way are you coming?

WHY DOES SHE WEEP?

Hush then
why do you cry?
It's you and me
the same as before.

If you hear a rustle
it's only a rabbit
gone back to his hole
in a bustle.

If something stirs in the branches
overhead, it will be a squirrel moving
uneasily, disturbed by the stress
of our loving.

Why should you cry then?
Are you afraid of God
in the dark?

I'm not afraid of God.
Let him come forth.
If he is hiding in the cover
let him come forth.

Now in the cool of the day
it is we who walk in the trees
and call to God "Where art thou?"
And it is he who hides.

Why do you cry?
My heart is bitter.
Let God come forth to justify
himself now.

Why do you cry?
Is it Wehmut, ist dir weh?
Weep then, yea
for the abomination of our old righteousness,

We have done wrong
many times;
but this time we begin to do right.

Weep then, weep
for the abomination of our past righteousness.
God will keep
hidden, he won't come forth.

GIORNO DEI MORTI

Along the avenue of cypresses
All in their scarlet cloaks, and surplices
Of linen go the chanting choristers,
The priests in gold and black, the villagers. . . .

And all along the path to the cemetery
The round dark heads of men crowd silently,
And black-scarved faces of women-folk, wistfully
Watch at the banner of death, and the mystery.

And at the foot of a grave a father stands
With sunken head, and forgotten, folded hands;
And at the foot of a grave a mother kneels
With pale shut face, nor either hears nor feels

The coming of the chanting choristers
Between the avenue of cypresses,
The silence of the many villagers,
The candle-flames beside the surplices.

ALL SOULS

They are chanting now the service of All the Dead
And the village folk outside in the burying ground
Listen—except those who strive with their dead,
Reaching out in anguish, yet unable quite to touch them:

Those villagers isolated at the grave
Where the candles burn in the daylight, and the painted wreaths
Are propped on end, there, where the mystery starts.

The naked candles burn on every grave.
On your grave, in England, the weeds grow.

But I am your naked candle burning,
And that is not your grave, in England,
The world is your grave.
And my naked body standing on your grave
Upright towards heaven is burning off to you
Its flame of life, now and always, till the end.

It is my offering to you; every day is All Souls' Day.

I forget you, have forgotten you.
I am busy only at my burning,
I am busy only at my life.
But my feet are on your grave, planted.
And when I lift my face, it is a flame that goes up
To the other world, where you are now.
But I am not concerned with you.
I have forgotten you.

I am a naked candle burning on your grave.

LADY WIFE

Ah yes, I know you well, a sojourner
    At the hearth;
I know right well the marriage ring you wear,
    And what it's worth.

The angels came to Abraham, and they stayed
    In his house awhile;
So you to mine, I imagine; yes, happily
    Condescend to be vile.

I see you all the time, you bird-blithe, lovely
    Angel in disguise.
I see right well how I ought to be grateful,
    Smitten with reverent surprise.

Listen, I have no use
    For so rare a visit;
Mine is a common devil's
    Requisite.

Rise up and go, I have no use for you
    And your blithe, glad mien.
No angels here, for me no goddesses,
    Nor any Queen.

Put ashes on your head, put sackcloth on
    And learn to serve.
You have fed me with your sweetness, now I am sick,
    As I deserve.

Queens, ladies, angels, women rare,
    I have had enough.
Put sackcloth on, be crowned with powdery ash,
    Be common stuff.

And serve now woman, serve, as a woman should,
    Implicitly.
Since I must serve and struggle with the imminent
    Mystery.

Serve then, I tell you, add your strength to mine
    Take on this doom.
What are you by yourself, do you think, and what
    The mere fruit of your womb?

What is the fruit of your womb then, you mother, you queen,
    When it falls to the ground?
Is it more than the apples of Sodom you scorn so, the men
    Who abound?

Bring forth the sons of your womb then, and put them
    Into the fire
Of Sodom that covers the earth; bring them forth
    From the womb of your precious desire.

You woman most holy, you mother, you being beyond
    Question or diminution,
Add yourself up, and your seed, to the nought
    Of your last solution.

BOTH SIDES OF THE MEDAL

And because you love me
think you you do not hate me?
Ha, since you love me
to ecstasy
it follows you hate me to ecstasy.

124

Because when you hear me
go down the road outside the house
you must come to the window to watch me go,
do you think it is pure worship?

Because, when I sit in the room,
here, in my own house,
and you want to enlarge yourself with this friend of mine,
such a friend as he is,
yet you cannot get beyond your awareness of me
you are held back by my being in the same world with you,
do you think it is bliss alone?
sheer harmony?

No doubt if I were dead, you must
reach into death after me,
but would not your hate reach even more madly than your love?
your impassioned, unfinished hate?

Since you have a passion for me,
as I for you,
does not that passion stand in your way like a Balaam's ass?
and am I not Balaam's ass
golden-mouthed occasionally?
But mostly, do you not detest my bray?

Since you are confined in the orbit of me
do you not loathe the confinement?
Is not even the beauty and peace of an orbit
an intolerable prison to you,
as it is to everybody?

But we will learn to submit
each of us to the balanced, eternal orbit
wherein we circle on our fate
in strange conjunction.

What is chaos, my love?
It is not freedom.
A disarray of falling stars coming to nought.

LOGGERHEADS

Please yourself how you have it.
Take my words, and fling
Them down on the counter roundly;
See if they ring.

Sift my looks and expressions,
And see what proportion there is
Of sand in my doubtful sugar
Of verities.

Have a real stock-taking
Of my manly breast;
Find out if I'm sound or bankrupt,
Or a poor thing at best.

For I am quite indifferent
To your dubious state,
As to whether you've found a fortune
In me, or a flea-bitten fate.

Make a good investigation
Of all that is there,
And then, if it's worth it, be grateful—
If not then despair.

If despair is our portion
Then let us despair.
Let us make for the weeping willow.
I don't care.

DECEMBER NIGHT

Take off your cloak and your hat
And your shoes, and draw up at my hearth
Where never woman sat.

I have made the fire up bright;
Let us leave the rest in the dark
And sit by firelight.

The wine is warm in the hearth;
The flickers come and go.
I will warm your feet with kisses
Until they glow.

NEW YEAR'S EVE

There are only two things now,
The great black night scooped out
And this fire-glow.

This fire-glow, the core,
And we the two ripe pips
That are held in store.

Listen, the darkness rings
As it circulates round our fire.
Take off your things.

Your shoulders, your bruised throat
Your breasts, your nakedness!
This fiery coat!

As the darkness flickers and dips,
As the firelight falls and leaps
From your feet to your lips!

NEW YEAR'S NIGHT

Now you are mine, to-night at last I say it;
You're a dove I have bought for sacrifice,
And to-night I slay it.

Here in my arms my naked sacrifice!
Death, do you hear, in my arms I am bringing
My offering, bought at great price.

She's a silvery dove worth more than all I've got.
Now I offer her up to the ancient, inexorable God,
Who knows me not.

Look, she's a wonderful dove, without blemish or spot!
I sacrifice all in her, my last of the world,
Pride, strength, all the lot.

All, all on the altar! And death swooping down
Like a falcon. 'Tis God has taken the victim;
I have won my renown.

VALENTINE'S NIGHT

You shadow and flame,
You interchange,
You death in the game!

Now I gather you up,
Now I put you back
Like a poppy in its cup.

And so, you are a maid
Again, my darling, but new,
Unafraid.

My love, my blossom, a child
Almost! The flower in the bud
Again, undefiled.

And yet, a woman, knowing
All, good, evil, both
In one blossom blowing.

BIRTH NIGHT

This fireglow is a red womb
In the night, where you're folded up
On your doom.

And the ugly, brutal years
Are dissolving out of you,
And the stagnant tears.

I the great vein that leads
From the night to the source of you,
Which the sweet blood feeds.

New phase in the germ of you;
New sunny streams of blood
Washing you through.

You are born again of me.
I, Adam, from the veins of me
The Eve that is to be.

What has been long ago
Grows dimmer, we both forget,
We no longer know.

You are lovely, your face is soft
Like a flower in bud
On a mountain croft.

This is Noël for me.
To-night is a woman born
Of the man in me.

RABBIT SNARED IN THE NIGHT

Why do you spurt and sprottle
like that, bunny?
Why should I want to throttle
you, bunny?

Yes, bunch yourself between
my knees and lie still.
Lie on me with a hot, plumb, live weight,
heavy as a stone, passive,
yet hot, waiting.

What are you waiting for?
What are you waiting for?
What is the hot, plumb weight of your desire on me?
You have a hot, unthinkable desire of me, bunny.

What is that spark
glittering at me on the unutterable darkness
of your eye, bunny?
The finest splinter of a spark
that you throw off, straight on the tinder of my nerves!

It sets up a strange fire,
a soft, most unwarrantable burning
a bale-fire mounting, mounting up in me.

'Tis not of me, bunny.
It was you engendered it,
with that fine, demoniacal spark
you jetted off your eye at me.

I did not want it,
this furnace, this draught-maddened fire
which mounts up my arms
making them swell with turgid, ungovernable strength.

'Twas not *I* that wished it,
that my fingers should turn into these flames
avid and terrible
that they are at this moment.

It must have been *your* inbreathing, gaping desire
that drew this red gush in me;
I must be reciprocating *your* vacuous, hideous passion.

It must be the want in you
that has drawn this terrible draught of white fire
up my veins as up a chimney.

It must be you who desire
this intermingling of the black and monstrous fingers of Moloch
in the blood-jets of your throat.

Come, you shall have your desire,
since already I am implicated with you
in your strange lust.

PARADISE RE-ENTERED

Through the strait gate of passion,
Between the bickering fire
Where flames of fierce love tremble
On the body of fierce desire:

To the intoxication,
The mind, fused down like a bead,
Flees in its agitation
The flames' stiff speed:

At last to calm incandescence,
Burned clean by remorseless hate,
Now, at the day's renascence
We approach the gate.

Now, from the darkened spaces
Of fear, and of frightened faces,
Death, in our awful embraces
Approached and passed by;

We near the flame-burnt porches
Where the brands of the angels, like torches
Whirl,—in these perilous marches
Pausing to sigh;

We look back on the withering roses,
The stars, in their sun-dimmed closes,
Where 'twas given us to repose us
Sure on our sanctity;

Beautiful, candid lovers,
Burnt out of our earthy covers,
We might have nestled like plovers
In the fields of eternity.

There, sure in sinless being,
All-seen, and then all-seeing,
In us life unto death agreeing,
We might have lain.

But we storm the angel-guarded
Gates of the long-discarded,
Garden, which God has hoarded
Against our pain.

The Lord of Hosts, and the Devil
Are left on Eternity's level
Field, and as victors we travel
To Eden home.

Back beyond good and evil
Return we. Eve dishevel
Your hair for the bliss-drenched revel
On our primal loam.

SPRING MORNING

Ah, through the open door
Is there an almond tree
Aflame with blossom!
    —Let us fight no more.

Among the pink and blue
Of the sky and the almond flowers
A sparrow flutters.
    —We have come through,

It is really spring!—See,
When he thinks himself alone
How he bullies the flowers.
    —Ah, you and me

How happy we'll be!—See him
He clouts the tufts of flowers
In his impudence.
    —But, did you dream

It would be so bitter? Never mind
It is finished, the spring is here.
And we're going to be summer-happy
    And summer-kind.

We have died, we have slain and been slain,
We are not our old selves any more.
I feel new and eager
    To start again.

It is gorgeous to live and forget.
And to feel quite new.
See the bird in the flowers?—he's making
    A rare to-do!

He thinks the whole blue sky
Is much less than the bit of blue egg
He's got in his nest—we'll be happy
    You and I, I and you.

With nothing to fight any more—
In each other, at least.
See, how gorgeous the world is
    Outside the door!

SAN GAUDENZIO

WEDLOCK

I

Come, my little one, closer up against me,
Creep right up, with your round head pushed in my breast.

How I love all of you! Do you feel me wrap you
Up with myself and my warmth, like a flame round the wick?

And how I am not at all, except a flame that mounts off you.
Where I touch you, I flame into being;—but is it me, or you?

That round head pushed in my chest, like a nut in its socket,
And I the swift bracts that sheathe it: those breasts, those thighs and
        knees,

Those shoulders so warm and smooth: I feel that I
Am a sunlight upon them, that shines them into being.

But how lovely to be you! Creep closer in, that
I am more.
I spread over you! How lovely, your round head, your arms,

Your breasts, your knees and feet! I feel that we
Are a bonfire of oneness, me flame flung leaping round you,
You the core of the fire, crept into me.

II

And oh, my little one, you whom I enfold,
How quaveringly I depend on you, to keep me alive,
Like a flame on a wick!

I, the man who enfolds you and holds you close,
How my soul cleaves to your bosom as I clasp you,
The very quick of my being!

Suppose you didn't want me! I should sink down
Like a light that has no sustenance
And sinks low.

Cherish me, my tiny one, cherish me who enfold you.
Nourish me, and endue me, I am only of you,
I am your issue.

How full and big like a robust, happy flame
When I enfold you, and you creep into me,
And my life is fierce at its quick
Where it comes off you!

III

My little one, my big one,
My bird, my brown sparrow in my breast.
My squirrel clutching in to me;
My pigeon, my little one, so warm
So close, breathing so still.

My little one, my big one,
I, who am so fierce and strong, enfolding you,
If you start away from my breast, and leave me,
How suddenly I shall go down into nothing
Like a flame that falls of a sudden.

And you will be before me, tall and towering,
And I shall be wavering uncertain
Like a sunken flame that grasps for support.

IV

But now I am full and strong and certain
With you there firm at the core of me
Keeping me.

How sure I feel, how warm and strong and happy
For the future! How sure the future is within me;
I am like a seed with a perfect flower enclosed.

I wonder what it will be,
What will come forth of us.
What flower, my love?

No matter, I am so happy,
I feel like a firm, rich, healthy root,
Rejoicing in what is to come.

How I depend on you utterly
My little one, my big one!
How everything that will be, will not be of me,
Nor of either of us,
But of both of us.

V

And think, there will something come forth from us.
We two, folded so small together,
There will something come forth from us.
Children, acts, utterance
Perhaps only happiness.

Perhaps only happiness will come forth from us.
Old sorrow, and new happiness.
Only that one newness.

But that is all I want.
And I am sure of that.
We are sure of that.

VI

And yet all the while you are you, you are not me.
And I am I, I am never you.
How awfully distinct and far off from each other's being we are!

Yet I am glad.
I am so glad there is always you beyond my scope,
Something that stands over,
Something I shall never be,
That I shall always wonder over, and wait for,
Look for like the breath of life as long as I live,
Still waiting for you, however old you are, and I am,
I shall always wonder over you, and look for you.

And you will always be with me.
I shall never cease to be filled with newness,
Having you near me.

HISTORY

The listless beauty of the hour
When snow fell on the apple trees
And the wood-ash gathered in the fire
And we faced our first miseries.

Then the sweeping sunshine of noon
When the mountains like chariot cars
Were ranked to blue battle—and you and I
Counted our scars.

And then in a strange, grey hour
We lay mouth to mouth, with your face
Under mine like a star on the lake,
And I covered the earth, and all space.

The silent, drifting hours
Of morn after morn
And night drifting up to the night
Yet no pathway worn.

Your life, and mine, my love
Passing on and on, the hate
Fusing closer and closer with love
Till at length they mate.

THE CEARNE

SONG OF A MAN WHO HAS COME THROUGH

Not I, not I, but the wind that blows through me!
A fine wind is blowing the new direction of Time.
If only I let it bear me, carry me, if only it carry me!
If only I am sensitive, subtle, oh, delicate, a winged gift!
If only, most lovely of all, I yield myself and am borrowed
By the fine, fine wind that takes its course through the chaos of the
        world
Like a fine, an exquisite chisel, a wedge-blade inserted;
If only I am keen and hard like the sheer tip of a wedge
Driven by invisible blows,
The rock will split, we shall come at the wonder, we shall find the
        Hesperides.

Oh, for the wonder that bubbles into my soul,
I would be a good fountain, a good well-head,
Would blur no whisper, spoil no expression.

What is the knocking?
What is the knocking at the door in the night?
It is somebody wants to do us harm.

No, no, it is the three strange angels.
Admit them, admit them.

ONE WOMAN TO ALL WOMEN

I don't care whether I am beautiful to you
        You other women.
Nothing of me that you see is my own;
A man balances, bone unto bone
Balances, everything thrown
        In the scale, you other women.

You may look and say to yourselves, I do
        Not show like the rest.
My face may not please you, nor my stature; yet if you knew
How happy I am, how my heart in the wind rings true
Like a bell that is chiming, each stroke as a stroke falls due,
        You other women:

136

You would draw your mirror towards you, you would wish
      To be different.
There's the beauty you cannot see, myself and him
Balanced in glorious equilibrium,
The swinging beauty of equilibrium,
      You other women.

There's this other beauty, the way of the stars
      You straggling women.
If you knew how I swerve in peace, in the equipoise
With the man, if you knew how my flesh enjoys
The swinging bliss no shattering ever destroys
      You other women:

You would envy me, you would think me wonderful
      Beyond compare;
You would weep to be lapsing on such harmony
As carries me, you would wonder aloud that he
Who is so strange should correspond with me
      Everywhere.

You see he is different, he is dangerous,
      Without pity or love.
And yet how his separate being liberates me
And gives me peace! You cannot see
How the stars are moving in surety
      Exquisite, high above.

We move without knowing, we sleep, and we travel on,
      You other women.
And this is beauty to me, to be lifted and gone
In a motion human inhuman, two and one
Encompassed, and many reduced to none,
      You other women.

    KENSINGTON

        PEOPLE

The great gold apples of night
Hang from the street's long bough
      Dripping their light
On the faces that drift below,
On the faces that drift and blow
Down the night-time, out of sight
      In the wind's sad sough.

The ripeness of these apples of night
Distilling over me
      Makes sickening the white
Ghost-flux of faces that hie
Them endlessly, endlessly by
Without meaning or reason why
      They ever should be.

STREET LAMPS

Gold, with an innermost speck
Of silver, singing afloat
    Beneath the night,
Like balls of thistle-down
Wandering up and down
Over the whispering town
    Seeking where to alight!

Slowly, above the street
Above the ebb of feet
    Drifting in flight;
Still, in the purple distance
The gold of their strange persistence
As they cross and part and meet
    And pass out of sight!

The seed-ball of the sun
Is broken at last, and done
    Is the orb of day.
Now to the separate ends
Seed after day-seed wends
    A separate way.

No sun will ever rise
Again on the wonted skies
    In the midst of the spheres.
The globe of the day, over-ripe,
Is shattered at last beneath the stripe
Of the wind, and its oneness veers
    Out myriad-wise.

Seed after seed after seed
Drifts over the town, in its need
    To sink and have done;
To settle at last in the dark,
To bury its weary spark
    Where the end is begun.

Darkness, and depth of sleep,
Nothing to know or to weep
    Where the seed sinks in
To the earth of the under-night
Where all is silent, quite
Still, and the darknesses steep
    Out all the sin.

"SHE SAID AS WELL TO ME"

She said as well to me: "Why are you ashamed?
That little bit of your chest that shows between
the gap of your shirt, why cover it up?
Why shouldn't your legs and your good strong thighs
be rough and hairy?—I'm glad they are like that.
You are shy, you silly, you silly shy thing.
Men are the shyest creatures, they never will come
out of their covers. Like any snake
slipping into its bed of dead leaves, you hurry into your clothes.
And I love you so! Straight and clean and all of a piece is the body of a
    man,
such an instrument, a spade, like a spear, or an oar,
such a joy to me—"
So she laid her hands and pressed them down my sides,
so that I began to wonder over myself, and what I was.

She said to me: "What an instrument, your body!
single and perfectly distinct from everything else!
What a tool in the hands of the Lord!
Only God could have brought it to its shape.
It feels as if his handgrasp, wearing you
had polished you and hollowed you,
hollowed this groove in your sides, grasped you under the breasts
and brought you to the very quick of your form,
subtler than an old, soft-worn fiddle-bow.

"When I was a child, I loved my father's riding-whip
that he used so often.
I loved to handle it, it seemed like a near part of him.
So I did his pens, and the jasper seal on his desk.
Something seemed to surge through me when I touched them.

"So it is with you, but here
The joy I feel!
God knows what I feel, but it is joy!
Look, you are clean and fine and singled out!
I admire you so, you are beautiful: this clean sweep of your sides, this
    firmness, this hard mould!

I would die rather than have it injured with one scar.
I wish I could grip you like the fist of the Lord,
and have you—"

So she said, and I wondered,
feeling trammelled and hurt.
It did not make me free.

Now I say to her: "No tool, no instrument, no God!
Don't touch me and appreciate me.
It is an infamy.
You would think twice before you touched a weasel on a fence
as it lifts its straight white throat.
Your hand would not be so flig and easy.
Nor the adder we saw asleep with her head on her shoulder,
curled up in the sunshine like a princess;
when she lifted her head in delicate, startled wonder
you did not stretch forward to caress her
though she looked rarely beautiful
and a miracle as she glided delicately away, with such dignity.
And the young bull in the field, with his wrinkled, sad face,
you are afraid if he rises to his feet,
though he is all wistful and pathetic, like a monolith, arrested, static.

"Is there nothing in me to make you hesitate?
I tell you there is all these.
And why should you overlook them in me?—"

NEW HEAVEN AND EARTH

I

And so I cross into another world
shyly and in homage linger for an invitation
from this unknown that I would trespass on.

I am very glad, and all alone in the world,
all alone, and very glad, in a new world
where I am disembarked at last.

I could cry with joy, because I am in the new world, just ventured in.
I could cry with joy, and quite freely, there is nobody to know.

And whosoever the unknown people of this unknown world may be
they will never understand my weeping for joy to be adventuring
      among them
because it will still be a gesture of the old world I am making
which they will not understand, because it is quite, quite foreign to
      them.

II

I was so weary of the world
I was so sick of it
everything was tainted with myself,
skies, trees, flowers, birds, water,
people, houses, streets, vehicles, machines,
nations, armies, war, peace-talking,
work, recreation, governing, anarchy,
it was all tainted with myself, I knew it all to start with
because it was all myself.

When I gathered flowers, I knew it was myself plucking my own
      flowering.
When I went in a train, I knew it was myself travelling by my own
      invention.
When I heard the cannon of the war, I listened with my own ears to my
      own destruction.
When I saw the torn dead, I knew it was my own torn dead body.
It was all me, I had done it all in my own flesh.

III

I shall never forget the maniacal horror of it all in the end
when everything was me, I knew it all already, I anticipated it all in my
      soul
because I was the author and the result
I was the God and the creation at once;
creator, I looked at my creation;
created, I looked at myself, the creator:
it was a maniacal horror in the end.

I was a lover, I kissed the woman I loved,
and God of horror, I was kissing also myself.
I was a father and a begetter of children,
and oh, oh horror, I was begetting and conceiving in my own body.

IV

At last came death, sufficiency of death,
and that at last relieved me, I died.
I buried my beloved; it was good, I buried myself and was gone.
War came, and every hand raised to murder;
very good, very good, every hand raised to murder!
Very good, very good, I am a murderer!
It is good, I can murder and murder, and see them fall
the mutilated, horror-struck youths, a multitude
one on another, and then in clusters together
smashed, all oozing with blood, and burned in heaps
going up in a foetid smoke to get rid of them
the murdered bodies of youths and men in heaps
and heaps and heaps and horrible reeking heaps
till it is almost enough, till I am reduced perhaps;
thousands and thousands of gaping, hideous foul dead
that are youths and men and me
being burned with oil, and consumed in corrupt thick smoke, that rolls
and taints and blackens the sky, till at last it is dark, dark as night, or
          death, or hell
and I am dead, and trodden to nought in the smoke-sodden tomb;
dead and trodden to nought in the sour black earth
of the tomb; dead and trodden to nought, trodden to nought.

V

God, but it is good to have died and been trodden out
trodden to nought in sour, dead earth
quite to nought
absolutely to nothing
nothing
nothing
nothing.

For when it is quite, quite nothing, then it is everything.
When I am trodden quite out, quite, quite out
every vestige gone, then I am here
risen, and setting my foot on another world
risen, accomplishing a resurrection
risen, not born again, but risen, body the same as before,
new beyond knowledge of newness, alive beyond life
proud beyond inkling or furthest conception of pride
living where life was never yet dreamed of, nor hinted at
here, in the other world, still terrestrial
myself, the same as before, yet unaccountably new.

VI

I, in the sour black tomb, trodden to absolute death
I put out my hand in the night, one night, and my hand
touched that which was verily not me
verily it was not me.
Where I had been was a sudden blaze
a sudden flaring blaze!
So I put my hand out further, a little further
and I felt that which was not I,
it verily was not I
it was the unknown.

Ha, I was a blaze leaping up!
I was a tiger bursting into sunlight.
I was greedy, I was mad for the unknown.
I, new-risen, resurrected, starved from the tomb
starved from a life of devouring always myself
now here was I, new-awakened, with my hand stretching out
and touching the unknown, the real unknown, the unknown unknown.

My God, but I can only say
I touch, I feel the unknown!
I am the first comer!
Cortes, Pisarro, Columbus, Cabot, they are nothing, nothing!
I am the first comer!
I am the discoverer!
I have found the other world!

The unknown, the unknown!
I am thrown upon the shore.
I am covering myself with the sand.
I am filling my mouth with the earth.
I am burrowing my body into the soil.
The unknown, the new world!

VII

It was the flank of my wife
I touched with my hand, I clutched with my hand
rising, new-awakened from the tomb!
It was the flank of my wife
whom I married years ago
at whose side I have lain for over a thousand nights
and all that previous while, she was I, she was I;
I touched her, it was I who touched and I who was
touched.

Yet rising from the tomb, from the black oblivion
stretching out my hand, my hand flung like a drowned man's hand on a
        rock,
I touched her flank and knew I was carried by the current in death
over to the new world, and was climbing out on the shore,
risen, not to the old world, the old, changeless I, the old life,
wakened not to the old knowledge
but to a new earth, a new I, a new knowledge, a new world of time.

Ah no, I cannot tell you what it is, the new world
I cannot tell you the mad, astounded rapture of its discovery.
I shall be mad with delight before I have done,
and whosoever comes after will find me in the new world
a madman in rapture.

VIII

GREEN streams that flow from the innermost continent of the new
        world,
what are they?
Green and illumined and travelling for ever
dissolved with the mystery of the innermost heart of the continent
mystery beyond knowledge or endurance, so sumptuous
out of the well-heads of the new world.—
The other, she too has strange green eyes!
White sands and fruits unknown and perfumes that never
can blow across the dark seas to our usual world!
And land that beats with a pulse!
And valleys that draw close in love!
And strange ways where I fall into oblivion of uttermost living!—
Also she who is the other has strange-mounded breasts and strange
        sheer slopes, and white levels.

Sightless and strong oblivion in utter life takes possession of me!
The unknown, strong current of life supreme
drowns me and sweeps me away and holds me down
to the sources of mystery, in the depths,
extinguishes there my risen resurrected life
and kindles it further at the core of utter mystery.

    GREATHAM

ELYSIUM

I have found a place of loneliness
Lonelier than Lyonesse
Lovelier than Paradise;

Full of sweet stillness
That no noise can transgress
Never a lamp distress.

The full moon sank in state.
I saw her stand and wait
For her watchers to shut the gate.

Then I found myself in a wonderland
All of shadow and of bland
Silence hard to understand.

I waited therefore; then I knew
The presence of the flowers that grew
Noiseless, their wonder noiseless blew.

And flashing kingfishers that flew
In sightless beauty, and the few
Shadows the passing wild-beast threw.

And Eve approaching over the ground
Unheard and subtle, never a sound
To let me know that I was found.

Invisible the hands of Eve
Upon me travelling to reeve
Me from the matrix, to relieve

Me from the rest! Ah terribly
Between the body of life and me
Her hands slid in and set me free.

Ah, with a fearful, strange detection
She found the source of my subjection
To the All, and severed the connection.

Delivered helpless and amazed
From the womb of the All, I am waiting, dazed
For memory to be erased.

Then I shall know the Elysium
That lies outside the monstrous womb
Of time from out of which I come.

MANIFESTO

I

A woman has given me strength and affluence.
Admitted!

All the rocking wheat of Canada, ripening now,
has not so much of strength as the body of one woman
sweet in ear, nor so much to give
though it feed nations.

Hunger is the very Satan.
The fear of hunger is Moloch, Belial, the horrible God.
It is a fearful thing to be dominated by the fear of hunger.

Not bread alone, not the belly nor the thirsty throat.
I have never yet been smitten through the belly, with the lack of bread,
no, nor even milk and honey.

The fear of the want of these things seems to be quite left out of me.
For so much, I thank the good generations of mankind.

II

And the sweet, constant, balanced heat
of the suave sensitive body, the hunger for this
has never seized me and terrified me.
Here again, man has been good in his legacy to us, in these two primary
                instances.

III

Then the dumb, aching, bitter, helpless need,
the pining to be initiated,
to have access to the knowledge that the great dead
have opened up for us, to know, to satisfy
the great and dominant hunger of the mind;
man's sweetest harvest of the centuries, sweet, printed books,
bright, glancing, exquisite corn of many a stubborn
glebe in the upturned darkness;
I thank mankind with passionate heart
that I just escaped the hunger for these,

that they were given when I needed them,
because I am the son of man.

I have eaten, and drunk, and warmed and clothed my body,
I have been taught the language of understanding,
I have chosen among the bright and marvellous books,
like any prince, such stores of the world's supply
were open to me, in the wisdom and goodness of man.
So far, so good.
Wise, good provision that makes the heart swell with love!

IV

But then came another hunger
very deep, and ravening;
the very body's body crying out
with a hunger more frightening, more profound
than stomach or throat or even the mind;
redder than death, more clamorous.

The hunger for the woman. Alas,
it is so deep a Moloch, ruthless and strong,
'tis like the unutterable name of the dread Lord,
not to be spoken aloud.
Yet there it is, the hunger which comes upon us,
which we must learn to satisfy with pure, real satisfaction;
or perish, there is no alternative.

I thought it was woman, indiscriminate woman,
mere female adjunct of what I was.
Ah, that was torment hard enough
and a thing to be afraid of,
a threatening, torturing, phallic Moloch.

A woman fed that hunger in me at last.
What many women cannot give, one woman can;
so I have known it.

She stood before me like riches that were mine.
Even then, in the dark, I was tortured, ravening, unfree,
Ashamed, and shameful, and vicious.
A man is so terrified of strong hunger;
and this terror is the root of all cruelty.
She loved me, and stood before me, looking to me.
How could I look, when I was mad? I looked sideways, furtively,
being mad with voracious desire.

V

This comes right at last.
When a man is rich, he loses at last the hunger fear.
I lost at last the fierceness that fears it will starve.
I could put my face at last between her breasts
and know that they were given for ever
that I should never starve
never perish;
I had eaten of the bread that satisfies
and my body's body was appeased,
there was peace and richness,
fulfilment.

Let them praise desire who will,
but only fulfilment will do,
real fulfilment, nothing short.
It is our ratification
our heaven, as a matter of fact.
Immortality, the heaven, is only a projection of this strange but actual
        fulfilment,
here in the flesh.

So, another hunger was supplied,
and for this I have to thank one woman,
not mankind, for mankind would have prevented me;
but one woman,
and these are my red-letter thanksgivings.

VI

To be, or not to be, is still the question.
This ache for being is the ultimate hunger.
And for myself, I can say "almost, almost, oh, very nearly."
Yet something remains.
Something shall not always remain.
For the main already is fulfilment.

What remains in me, is to be known even as I know.
I know her now: or perhaps, I know my own limitation against her.

Plunging as I have done, over, over the brink
I have dropped at last headlong into nought, plunging upon sheer hard
        extinction;
I have come, as it were, not to know,
died, as it were; ceased from knowing; surpassed myself.
What can I say more, except that I know what it is to surpass myself?

It is a kind of death which is not death.
It is going a little beyond the bounds.
How can one speak, where there is a dumbness on one's mouth?
I suppose, ultimately she is all beyond me,
she is all not-me, ultimately.
It is that that one comes to.
A curious agony, and a relief, when I touch that which is not me in any
       sense,
it wounds me to death with my own not-being; definite, inviolable
       limitation,
and something beyond, quite beyond, if you understand what that
       means.
It is the major part of being, this having surpassed oneself,
this having touched the edge of the beyond, and perished, yet not
       perished.

VII

I want her though, to take the same from me.
She touches me as if I were herself, her own.
She has not realized yet, that fearful thing, that I am the other,
she thinks we are all of one piece.
It is painfully untrue.

I want her to touch me at last, ah, on the root and quick of my darkness
and perish on me, as I have perished on her.

Then, we shall be two and distinct, we shall have each our separate
       being.
And that will be pure existence, real liberty.
Till then, we are confused, a mixture, unresolved, unextricated one
       from the other.
It is in pure, unutterable resolvedness, distinction
of being, that one is free,
not in mixing, merging, not in similarity.
When she has put her hand on my secret, darkest
sources, the darkest outgoings,
when it has struck home to her, like a death, "this is *him*!"
she has no part in it, no part whatever,
it is the terrible *other*,
when she knows the fearful *other flesh*, ah, darkness unfathomable and
       fearful, contiguous and concrete,
when she is slain against me, and lies in a heap
like one outside the house,
when she passes away as I have passed away
being pressed up against the *other*,
then I shall be glad, I shall not be confused with her,

I shall be cleared, distinct, single as if burnished in silver,
having no adherence, no adhesion anywhere,
one clear, burnished, isolated being, unique,
and she also, pure, isolated, complete,
two of us, unutterably distinguished, and in unutterable conjunction.

Then we shall be free, freer than angels, ah, perfect.

VIII

After that, there will only remain that all men
detach themselves and become unique,
that we are all detached, moving in freedom more
than the angels,
conditioned only by our own pure single being,
having no laws but the laws of our own being.

Every human being will then be like a flower, untrammelled.
Every movement will be direct.
Only to be will be such delight, we cover our faces when we think of it
lest our faces betray us to some untimely fiend.

Every man himself, and therefore, a surpassing singleness of mankind.
The blazing tiger will spring upon the deer, undimmed,
the hen will nestle over her chickens,
we shall love, we shall hate,
but it will be like music, sheer utterance,
issuing straight out of the unknown,
the lightning and the rainbow appearing in us unbidden, unchecked,
like ambassadors.

We shall not look before and after.
We shall *be, now.*
We shall know in full.
We, the mystic NOW.

ZENNOR

AUTUMN RAIN

The plane leaves
fall black and wet
on the lawn;

The cloud sheaves
in heaven's fields set
droop and are drawn

in falling seeds of rain;
the seed of heaven
on my face

falling—I hear again
like echoes even
that softly pace

Heaven's muffled floor,
the winds that tread
out all the grain

of tears, the store
harvested
in the sheaves of pain

caught up aloft:
the sheaves of dead
men that are slain

now winnowed soft
on the floor of heaven;
manna invisible

of all the pain
here to us given;
finely divisible
falling as rain.

FROST FLOWERS

It is not long since, here among all these folk
in London, I should have held myself
of no account whatever,
but should have stood aside and made them way
thinking that they, perhaps,
had more right than I—for who was I?

Now I see them just the same, and watch them.
But of what account do I hold them?

Especially the young women. I look at them
as they dart and flash
before the shops, like wagtails on the edge of a pool.

If I pass them close, or any man,
like sharp, slim wagtails they flash a little aside
pretending to avoid us; yet all the time
calculating.

They think that we adore them—alas, would it were true!

Probably they think all men adore them,
howsoever they pass by.

What is it, that, from their faces fresh as spring,
such fair, fresh, alert, first-flower faces,
like lavender crocuses, snowdrops, like Roman hyacinths,
scyllas and yellow-haired hellebore, jonquils, dim anemones,
even the sulphur auriculas,
flowers that come first from the darkness, and feel cold to the touch,
flowers scentless or pungent, ammoniacal almost;
what is it, that, from the faces of the fair young women
comes like a pungent scent, a vibration beneath
that startles me, alarms me, stirs up a repulsion?

They are the issue of acrid winter, these first-flower young women;
their scent is lacerating and repellant,
it smells of burning snow, of hot-ache,
of earth, winter-pressed, strangled in corruption;
it is the scent of the fiery-cold dregs of corruption,
when destruction soaks through the mortified, decomposing earth,
and the last fires of dissolution burn in the bosom of the ground.

They are the flowers of ice-vivid mortification,
thaw-cold, ice-corrupt blossoms,
with a loveliness I loathe;
for what kind of ice-rotten, hot-aching heart must they need to root in!

CRAVING FOR SPRING

I wish it were spring in the world.

Let it be spring!
Come, bubbling, surging tide of sap!
Come, rush of creation!
Come, life! surge through this mass of mortification!
Come, sweep away these exquisite, ghastly first-flowers,
which are rather last-flowers!
Come, thaw down their cool portentousness, dissolve them:
snowdrops, straight, death-veined exhalations of white and purple
        crocuses,

flowers of the penumbra, issue of corruption, nourished in
          mortification,
jets of exquisite finality;
Come, spring, make havoc of them!

I trample on the snowdrops, it gives me pleasure to tread down the
          jonquils,
to destroy the chill Lent lilies;
for I am sick of them, their faint-bloodedness,
slow-blooded, icy-fleshed, portentous.

I want the fine, kindling wine-sap of spring,
gold, and of inconceivably fine, quintessential brightness,
rare almost as beams, yet overwhelmingly potent,
strong like the greatest force of world-balancing.

This is the same that picks up the harvest of wheat
and rocks it, tons of grain, on the ripening wind;
the same that dangles the globe-shaped pleiads of fruit
temptingly in mid-air, between a playful thumb and finger;
oh, and suddenly, from out of nowhere, whirls the pear-bloom,
upon us, and apple- and almond- and apricot-and quince-blossom,
storms and cumulus clouds of all imaginable blossom
about our bewildered faces,
though we do not worship.

I wish it were spring
cunningly blowing on the fallen sparks, odds and ends of the old,
          scattered fire,
and kindling shapely little conflagrations
curious long-legged foals, and wide-eared calves, and naked sparrow-
          bubs.

I wish that spring
would start the thundering traffic of feet
new feet on the earth, beating with impatience.

I wish it were spring, thundering delicate, tender spring.
I wish these brittle, frost-lovely flowers of passionate, mysterious
          corruption
were not yet to come still more from the still-flickering discontent.

Oh, in the spring, the bluebell bows him down for very exuberance,
exulting with secret warm excess,
bowed down with his inner magnificence!

Oh, yes, the gush of spring is strong enough
to toss the globe of earth like a ball on a water-jet dancing sportfully;
as you see a tiny celluloid ball tossing on a squint of water
for men to shoot at, penny-a-time, in a booth at a fair.

The gush of spring is strong enough
to play with the globe of earth like a ball on a fountain;
At the same time it opens the tiny hands of the hazel
with such infinite patience.

The power of the rising, golden, all-creative sap could take the earth
and heave it off among the stars, into the invisible;
the same sets the throstle at sunset on a bough
singing against the blackbird;
comes out in the hesitating tremor of the primrose,
and betrays its candour in the round white strawberry flower,
is dignified in the foxglove, like a Red-Indian brave.

Ah come, come quickly, spring!
Come and lift us towards our culmination, we myriads;
we who have never flowered, like patient cactuses.
Come and lift us to our end, to blossom, bring us to our summer
we who are winter-weary in the winter of the world.
Come making the chaffinch nests hollow and cosy,
come and soften the willow buds till they are puffed and furred,
then blow them over with gold.
Come and cajole the gawky colt's-foot flowers.

Come quickly, and vindicate us
against too much death.
Come quickly, and stir the rotten globe of the world from within,
burst it with germination, with world anew.
Come now, to us, your adherents, who cannot flower from the ice.
All the world gleams with the lilies of Death the Unconquerable,
but come, give us our turn.
Enough of the virgins and lilies, of passionate, suffocating perfume of
            corruption,
no more narcissus perfume, lily harlots, the blades of sensation
piercing the flesh to blossom of death.
Have done, have done with this shuddering, delicious business
of thrilling ruin in the flesh, of pungent passion, of rare, death-edged
            ecstasy.
Give us our turn, give us a chance, let our hour strike,
O soon, soon!

Let the darkness turn violet with rich dawn.
Let the darkness be warmed, warmed through to a ruddy violet,
incipient purpling towards summer in the world of the heart of man.

Are the violets already here!
Show me! I tremble so much to hear it, that even now
on the threshold of spring, I fear I shall die.
Show me the violets that are out.

Oh, if it be true, and the living darkness of the blood of man is purpling
        with violets,
if the violets are coming out from under the rack of men, winter-rotten
        and fallen
we shall have spring.
Pray not to die on this Pisgah blossoming with violets.
Pray to live through.

If you catch a whiff of violets from the darkness of the shadow of man
it will be spring in the world,
it will be spring in the world of the living;
wonderment organising itself, heralding itself with the violets,
stirring of new seasons.

Ah, do not let me die on the brink of such anticipation!
Worse, let me not deceive myself.

    ZENNOR

NEW POEMS (1918)

APPREHENSION

And all hours long, the town
  Roars like a beast in a cave
That is wounded there
And like to drown;
  While days rush, wave after wave
On its lair.

An invisible woe unseals
  The flood, so it passes beyond
All bounds: the great old city
Recumbent roars as it feels
  The foamy paw of the pond
Reach from immensity.

But all that it can do
  Now, as the tide rises,
Is to listen and hear the grim
Waves crash like thunder through
  The splintered streets, hear noises
Roll hollow in the interim.

COMING AWAKE

When I woke, the lake-lights were quivering on the wall,
  The sunshine swam in a shoal across and across,
And a hairy, big bee hung over the primulas
  In the window, his body black fur, and the sound of him cross.

There was something I ought to remember: and yet
  I did not remember. Why should I? The running lights
And the airy primulas, oblivious
  Of the impending bee—they were fair enough sights.

FROM A COLLEGE WINDOW

The glimmer of the limes, sun-heavy, sleeping,
  Goes trembling past me up the College wall.
Below, the lawn, in soft blue shade is keeping,
  The daisy-froth quiescent, softly in thrall.

Beyond the leaves that overhang the street,
    Along the flagged, clean pavement summer-white,
Passes the world with shadows at their feet
    Going left and right.

Remote, although I hear the beggar's cough,
    See the woman's twinkling fingers tend him a coin,
I sit absolved, assured I am better off
    Beyond a world I never want to join.

FLAPPER

Love has crept out of her sealéd heart
As a field-bee, black and amber,
Breaks from the winter-cell, to clamber
Up the warm grass where the sunbeams start.

Mischief has come in her dawning eyes,
And a glint of coloured iris brings
Such as lies along the folded wings
Of the bee before he flies.

Who, with a ruffling, careful breath,
Has opened the wings of the wild young sprite?
Has fluttered her spirit to stumbling flight
In her eyes, as a young bee stumbleth?

Love makes the burden of her voice.
    The hum of his heavy, staggering wings
    Sets quivering with wisdom the common things
That she says, and her words rejoice.

BIRDCAGE WALK

When the wind blows her veil
    And uncovers her laughter
I cease, I turn pale.
When the wind blows her veil
From the woes I bewail
    Of love and hereafter:
When the wind blows her veil
I cease, I turn pale.

LETTER FROM TOWN: THE ALMOND TREE

You promised to send me some violets. Did you forget?
   White ones and blue ones from under the orchard hedge?
   Sweet dark purple, and white ones mixed for a pledge
Of our early love that hardly has opened yet.

Here there's an almond tree—you have never seen
   Such a one in the north—it flowers on the street, and I stand
   Every day by the fence to look up for the flowers that expand
At rest in the blue, and wonder at what they mean.

Under the almond tree, the happy lands
   Provence, Japan, and Italy repose,
   And passing feet are chatter and clapping of those
Who play around us, country girls clapping their hands.

You, my love, the foremost, in a flowered gown,
   All your unbearable tenderness, you with the laughter
   Startled upon your eyes now so wide with hereafter,
You with loose hands of abandonment hanging down.

FLAT SUBURBS, S.W., IN THE MORNING

The new red houses spring like plants
   In level rows
Of reddish herbage that bristles and slants
   Its square shadows.

The pink young houses show one side bright
   Flatly assuming the sun,
And one side shadow, half in sight,
   Half-hiding the pavement-run;

Where hastening creatures pass intent
   On their level way,
Threading like ants that can never relent
   And have nothing to say.

Bare stems of street-lamps stiffly stand
   At random, desolate twigs,
To testify to a blight on the land
   That has stripped their sprigs.

THIEF IN THE NIGHT

Last night a thief came to me
  And struck at me with something dark.
I cried, but no one could hear me,
  I lay dumb and stark.

When I awoke this morning
  I could find no trace;
Perhaps 'twas a dream of warning,
  For I've lost my peace.

LETTER FROM TOWN: ON A GREY EVENING IN MARCH

The clouds are pushing in grey reluctance slowly northward to you,
  While north of them all, at the farthest ends, stands one bright-
      bosomed, aglance
With fire as it guards the wild north cloud-coasts, red-fire seas running
    through
  The rocks where ravens flying to windward melt as a well-shot lance.

You should be out by the orchard, where violets secretly darken the
    earth,
  Or there in the woods of the twilight, with northern wind-flowers
      shaken astir.
Think of me here in the library, trying and trying a song that is worth
  Tears and swords to my heart, arrows no armour will turn or deter.

You tell me the lambs have come, they lie like daisies white in the
    grass
  Of the dark-green hills; new calves in shed; peewits turn after the
      plough—
It is well for you. For me the navvies work in the road where I pass
  And I want to smite in anger the barren rock of each waterless brow.

Like the sough of a wind that is caught up high in the mesh of the
    budding trees,
  A sudden car goes sweeping past, and I strain my soul to hear
The voice of the furtive triumphant engine as it rushes past like a
    breeze,
  To hear on its mocking triumphance unwitting the after-echo of fear.

SUBURBS ON A HAZY DAY

O stiffly shapen houses that change not,
  What conjuror's cloth was thrown across you, and raised
To show you thus transfigured, changed,
  Your stuff all gone, your menace almost rased?

Such resolute shapes, so harshly set
  In hollow blocks and cubes deformed, and heaped
In void and null profusion, how is this?
  In what strong *aqua regia* now are you steeped?

That you lose the brick-stuff out of you
  And hover like a presentment, fading faint
And vanquished, evaporate away
  To leave but only the merest possible taint!

HYDE PARK AT NIGHT, BEFORE THE WAR

Clerks

We have shut the doors behind us, and the velvet flowers of night
Lean about us scattering their pollen grains of golden light.

Now at last we lift our faces, and our faces come aflower
To the night that takes us willing, liberates us to the hour.

Now at last the ink and dudgeon passes from our fervent eyes
And out of the chambered weariness wanders a spirit abroad on its
      enterprise.

    Not too near and not too far
    Out of the stress of the crowd
    Music screams as elephants scream
    When they lift their trunks and scream aloud
    For joy of the night when masters are
        Asleep and adream.

    So here I hide in the Shalimar
    With a wanton princess slender and proud,
    And we swoon with kisses, swoon till we seem
    Two streaming peacocks gone in a cloud
    Of golden dust, with star after star
        On our stream.

GIPSY

I, the man with the red scarf,
   Will give thee what I have, this last week's earnings.
Take them, and buy thee a silver ring
   And wed me, to ease my yearnings.

For the rest, when thou art wedded
   I'll wet my brow for thee
With sweat, I'll enter a house for thy sake,
   Thou shalt shut doors on me.

TWO-FOLD

How gorgeous that shock of red lilies, and larkspur cleaving
All with a flash of blue!—when will she be leaving
Her room, where the night still hangs like a half-folded bat,
And passion unbearable seethes in the darkness, like must in a vat.

UNDER THE OAK

You, if you were sensible,
When I tell you the stars flash signals, each one dreadful,
You would not turn and answer me
"The night is wonderful."

Even you, if you knew
How this darkness soaks me through and through, and infuses
Unholy fear in my vapour, you would pause to distinguish
What hurts, from what amuses.

For I tell you
Beneath this powerful tree, my whole soul's fluid
Oozes away from me as a sacrifice steam
At the knife of a Druid.

Again I tell you, I bleed, I am bound with withies,
My life runs out.
I tell you my blood runs out on the floor of this oak,
Gout upon gout.

Above me springs the blood-born mistletoe
In the shady smoke.
But who are you, twittering to and fro
Beneath the oak?

What thing better are you, what worse?
What have you to do with the mysteries
Of this ancient place, of my ancient curse?
What place have you in my histories?

SIGH NO MORE

The cuckoo and the coo-dove's ceaseless calling,
                    Calling,
Of a meaningless monotony is palling
All my morning's pleasure in the sun-fleck-scattered wood.
May-blossom and blue bird's-eye flowers falling,
                    Falling
In a litter through the elm-tree shade are scrawling
Messages of true-love down the dust of the high-road.
I do not like to hear the gentle grieving,
                    Grieving
Of the she-dove in the blossom, still believing
Love will yet again return to her and make all good.

When I know that there must ever be deceiving,
                    Deceiving
Of the mournful constant heart, that while she's weaving
Her woes, her lover woos and sings within another wood.

Oh, boisterous the cuckoo shouts, forestalling,
                    Stalling
A progress down the intricate enthralling
By-paths where the wanton-headed flowers doff their hood.

And like a laughter leads me onward, heaving,
                    Heaving
A sigh among the shadows, thus retrieving
A decent short regret for that which once was very good.

LOVE STORM

Many roses in the wind
Are tapping at the window-sash.
A hawk is in the sky; his wings
Slowly begin to plash.

The roses with the west wind rapping
Are torn away, and a splash
Of red goes down the billowing air.

Still hangs the hawk, with the whole sky moving
Past him—only a wing-beat proving
The will that holds him there.

The daisies in the grass are bending,
The hawk has dropped, the wind is spending
All the roses, and unending
Rustle of leaves washes out the rending
Cry of a bird.

A red rose goes on the wind.—Ascending
The hawk his wind-swept way is wending
Easily down the sky. The daisies, sending
Strange white signals, seem intending
To show the place whence the scream was heard.

But, oh, my heart, what birds are piping!
A silver wind is hastily wiping
The face of the youngest rose.

And oh, my heart, cease apprehending!
The hawk is gone, a rose is tapping
The window-sash as the west-wind blows.

Knock, knock, 'tis no more than a red rose rapping,
And fear is a plash of wings.
What, then, if a scarlet rose goes flapping
Down the bright-grey ruin of things!

PARLIAMENT HILL IN THE EVENING

The houses fade in a melt of mist
    Blotching the thick, soiled air
With reddish places that still resist
    The Night's slow care.

The hopeless, wintry twilight fades,
    The city corrodes out of sight
As the body corrodes when death invades
    That citadel of delight.

Now verdigris smoulderings softly spread
    Through the shroud of the town, as slow
Night-lights hither and thither shed
    Their ghastly glow.

PICCADILLY CIRCUS AT NIGHT

Street-Walkers

When into the night the yellow light is roused like dust above the
    towns,
Or like a mist the moon has kissed from off a pool in the midst of the
    downs,

Our faces flower for a little hour pale and uncertain along the street,
Daisies that waken all mistaken white-spread in expectancy to meet

The luminous mist which the poor things wist was dawn arriving across
    the sky,
When dawn is far behind the star the dust-lit town has driven so high.

All the birds are folded in a silent ball of sleep,
All the flowers are faded from the asphalt isle in the sea,
Only we hard-faced creatures go round and round, and keep
The shores of this innermost ocean alive and illusory.

Wanton sparrows that twittered when morning looked in at their eyes
And the Cyprian's pavement-roses are gone, and now it is we
Flowers of illusion who shine in our gauds, make a Paradise
On the shores of this ceaseless ocean, gay birds of the town-dark sea.

TARANTELLA

Sad as he sits on the white sea-stone
And the suave sea chuckles, and turns to the moon,
And the moon significant smiles at the cliffs and the boulders.
He sits like a shade by the flood alone
While I dance a tarantella on the rocks, and the croon
Of my mockery mocks at him over the waves' bright shoulders.

What can I do but dance alone,
Dance to the sliding sea and the moon,
For the moon on my breast and the air on my limbs and the foam on my
    feet?
For surely this earnest man has none
Of the night in his soul, and none of the tune
Of the waters within him; only the world's old wisdom to bleat.

164

I wish a wild sea-fellow would come down the glittering shingle,
A soulless neckar, with winking seas in his eyes
And falling waves in his arms, and the lost soul's kiss
On his lips: I long to be soulless, I tingle
To touch the sea in the last surprise
Of fiery coldness, to be gone in a lost soul's bliss.

IN CHURCH

In the choir the boys are singing the hymn.
      The morning light on their lips
Moves in silver-moist flashes, in musical trim.

Sudden outside the high window, one crow
      Hangs in the air
And lights on a withered oak-tree's top of woe.

One bird, one blot, folded and still at the top
      Of the withered tree!—in the grail
Of crystal heaven falls one full black drop.

Like a soft full drop of darkness it seems to sway
      In the tender wine
Of our Sabbath, suffusing our sacred day.

PIANO

Softly, in the dusk, a woman is singing to me;
Taking me back down the vista of years, till I see
A child sitting under the piano, in the boom of the tingling strings
And pressing the small, poised feet of a mother who smiles as she
      sings.

In spite of myself, the insidious mastery of song
Betrays me back, till the heart of me weeps to belong
To the old Sunday evenings at home, with winter outside
And hymns in the cosy parlour, the tinkling piano our guide.

So now it is vain for the singer to burst into clamour
With the great black piano appassionato. The glamour
Of childish days is upon me, my manhood is cast
Down in the flood of remembrance, I weep like a child for the past.

EMBANKMENT AT NIGHT, BEFORE THE WAR

Charity

By the river
In the black wet night as the furtive rain slinks down,
Dropping and starting from sleep
Alone on a seat
A woman crouches.

I must go back to her.

I want to give her
Some money. Her hand slips out of the breast of her gown
Asleep. My fingers creep
Carefully over the sweet
Thumb-mound, into the palm's deep pouches.

So, the gift!

God, how she starts!
And looks at me, and looks in the palm of her hand!
And again at me!
I turn and run
Down the Embankment, run for my life.

But why?—why?

Because of my heart's
Beating like sobs, I come to myself, and stand
In the street spilled over splendidly
With wet, flat lights. What I've done
I know not, my soul is in strife.

The touch was on the quick. I want to forget.

PHANTASMAGORIA

Rigid sleeps the house in darkness, I alone
Like a thing unwarrantable cross the hall
And climb the stairs to find the group of doors
Standing angel-stern and tall.

I want my own room's shelter. But what is this
Throng of startled beings suddenly thrown
In confusion against my entry? Is it only the trees'
Large shadows from the outside street lamp blown?

Phantom to phantom leaning; strange women weep
Aloud, suddenly on my mind
Startling a fear unspeakable, as the shuddering wind
Breaks and sobs in the blind.

So like to women, tall strange women weeping!
Why continually do they cross the bed?
Why does my soul contract with unnatural fear?
I am listening! Is anything said?

Ever the long black figures swoop by the bed;
They seem to be beckoning, rushing away, and beckoning.
Whither then, whither, what is it, say
What is the reckoning.

Tall black Bacchae of midnight, why then, why
Do you rush to assail me?
Do I intrude on your rites nocturnal?
What should it avail me?

Is there some great Iacchos of these slopes
Suburban dismal?
Have I profaned some female mystery, orgies
Black and phantasmal?

NEXT MORNING

How have I wandered here to this vaulted room
In the house of life?—the floor was ruffled with gold
Last evening, and she who was softly in bloom,
Glimmered as flowers that in perfume at twilight unfold

For the flush of the night; whereas now the gloom
Of every dirty, must-besprinkled mould,
And damp old web of misery's heirloom
Deadens this day's grey-dropping arras-fold.

And what is this that floats on the undermist
Of the mirror towards the dusty grate, as if feeling
Unsightly its way to the warmth?—this thing with a list
To the left? this ghost like a candle swealing?

Pale-blurred, with two round black drops, as if it missed
Itself among everything else, here hungrily stealing
Upon me!—my own reflection!—explicit gist
Of my presence there in the mirror that leans from the ceiling!

Then will somebody square this shade with the being I know
I was last night, when my soul rang clear as a bell
And happy as rain in summer? Why should it be so?
What is there gone against me, why am I in hell?

PALIMPSEST OF TWILIGHT

Darkness comes out of the earth
    And swallows dip into the pallor of the west;
From the hay comes the clamour of children's mirth;
    Wanes the old palimpsest.

The night-stock oozes scent,
    And a moon-blue moth goes flittering by:
All that the worldly day has meant
    Wastes like a lie.

The children have forsaken their play;
    A single star in a veil of light
Glimmers: litter of day
    Is gone from sight.

EMBANKMENT AT NIGHT, BEFORE THE WAR

Outcasts

The night rain, dripping unseen,
Comes endlessly kissing my face and my hands.

The river, slipping between
Lamps, is rayed with golden bands
Half way down its heaving sides;
Revealed where it hides.

Under the bridge
Great electric cars
Sing through, and each with a floor-light racing along at its side.
Far off, oh, midge after midge
Drifts over the gulf that bars
The night with silence, crossing the lamp-touched tide.

At Charing Cross, here, beneath the bridge
Sleep in a row the outcasts,
Packed in a line with their heads against the wall.
Their feet, in a broken ridge
Stretch out on the way, and a lout casts
A look as he stands on the edge of this naked stall.

168

Beasts that sleep will cover
Their faces in their flank; so these
Have huddled rags or limbs on the naked sleep.
Save, as the tram-cars hover
Past with the noise of a breeze
And gleam as of sunshine crossing the low black heap,

Two naked faces are seen
Bare and asleep,
Two pale clots swept and swept by the light of the cars.
Foam-clots showing between
The long, low tidal-heap,
The mud-weed opening two pale, shadowless stars.

Over the pallor of only two faces
Passes the gallivant beam of the trams;
Shows in only two sad places
The white bare bone of our shams.

A little, bearded man, pale, peaked in sleeping,
With a face like a chickweed flower.
And a heavy woman, sleeping still keeping
Callous and dour.

Over the pallor of only two places
Tossed on the low, black, ruffled heap
Passes the light of the tram as it races
Out of the deep.

Eloquent limbs
In disarray
Sleep-suave limbs of a youth with long, smooth thighs
Hutched up for warmth; the muddy rims
Of trousers fray
On the thin bare shins of a man who uneasily lies.

The balls of five red toes
As red and dirty, bare
Young birds forsaken and left in a nest of mud—
Newspaper sheets enclose
Some limbs like parcels, and tear
When the sleeper stirs or turns on the ebb of the flood—

One heaped mound
Of a woman's knees
As she thrusts them upward under the ruffled skirt—
And a curious dearth of sound
In the presence of these
Wastrels that sleep on the flagstones without any hurt.

Over two shadowless, shameless faces
Stark on the heap
Travels the light as it tilts in its paces
Gone in one leap.

At the feet of the sleepers, watching,
Stand those that wait
For a place to lie down; and still as they stand, they sleep,
Wearily catching
The flood's slow gait
Like men who are drowned, but float erect in the deep.

Oh, the singing mansions,
Golden-lighted tall
Trams that pass, blown ruddily down the night!
The bridge on its stanchions
Stoops like a pall
To this human blight.

On the outer pavement, slowly,
Theatre people pass,
Holding aloft their umbrellas that flash and are bright
Like flowers of infernal moly
Over nocturnal grass
Wetly bobbing and drifting away on our sight.

And still by the rotten
Row of shattered feet,
Outcasts keep guard.
Forgotten,
Forgetting, till fate shall delete
One from the ward.

The factories on the Surrey side
Are beautifully laid in black on a gold-grey sky.
The river's invisible tide
Threads and thrills like ore that is wealth to the eye.
And great gold midges
Cross the chasm
At the bridges
Above intertwined plasm.

WINTER IN THE BOULEVARD

The frost has settled down upon the trees
And ruthlessly strangled off the fantasies
Of leaves that have gone unnoticed, swept like old
Romantic stories now no more to be told.

The trees down the boulevard stand naked in thought,
Their abundant summery wordage silenced, caught
In the grim undertow; naked the trees confront
Implacable winter's long, cross-questioning brunt.

Has some hand balanced more leaves in the depths of the twigs?
Some dim little efforts placed in the threads of the birch?—
It is only the sparrows, like dead black leaves on the sprigs,
Sitting huddled against the cerulean, one flesh with their perch.

The clear, cold sky coldly bethinks itself.
Like vivid thought the air spins bright, and all
Trees, birds, and earth, arrested in the after-thought
Awaiting the sentence out from the welkin brought.

SCHOOL ON THE OUTSKIRTS

How different, in the middle of snows, the great school rises red!
  A red rock silent and shadowless, clung round with clusters of
      shouting lads,
Some few dark-cleaving the doorway, souls that cling as the souls of
      the dead
  In stupor persist at the gates of life, obstinate dark monads.

This new red rock in a waste of white rises against the day
  With shelter now, and with blandishment, since the winds have had
      their way
And laid the desert horrific of silence and snow on the world of
      mankind,
  School now is the rock in this weary land the winter burns and makes
      blind.

SICKNESS

Waving slowly before me, pushed into the dark,
Unseen my hands explore the silence, drawing the bark
Of my body slowly behind.

Nothing to meet my fingers but the fleece of night
Invisible blinding my face and my eyes! What if in their flight
My hands should touch the door!

What if I suddenly stumble, and push the door
Open, and a great grey dawn swirls over my feet, before
I can draw back!

What if unwitting I set the door of eternity wide
And am swept away in the horrible dawn, am gone down the tide
Of eternal hereafter!

Catch my hands, my darling, between your breasts.
Take them away from their venture, before fate wrests
The meaning out of them.

EVERLASTING FLOWERS

Who do you think stands watching
    The snow-tops shining rosy
In heaven, now that the darkness
    Takes all but the tallest posy?

Who then sees the two-winged
    Boat down there, all alone
And asleep on the snow's last shadow,
    Like a moth on a stone?

The olive-leaves, light as gad-flies,
    Have all gone dark, gone black.
And now in the dark my soul to you
    Turns back.

To you, my little darling,
    To you, out of Italy.
For what is loveliness, my love,
    Save you have it with me!

So, there's an oxen wagon
  Comes darkly into sight:
A man with a lantern, swinging
  A little light.

What does he see, my darling
  Here by the darkened lake?
Here, in the sloping shadow
  The mountains make?

He says not a word, but passes,
  Staring at what he sees.
What ghost of us both do you think he saw
  Under the olive trees?

All the things that are lovely—
  The things you never knew—
I wanted to gather them one by one
  And bring them to you.

But never now, my darling
  Can I gather the mountain-tips
From the twilight like half-shut lilies
  To hold to your lips.

And never the two-winged vessel
  That sleeps below on the lake
Can I catch like a moth between my hands
  For you to take.

But hush, I am not regretting:
  It is far more perfect now.
I'll whisper the ghostly truth to the world
  And tell them how

I know you here in the darkness,
  How you sit in the throne of my eyes
At peace, and look out of the windows
  In glad surprise.

THE NORTH COUNTRY

In another country, black poplars shake themselves over a pond,
And rooks and the rising smoke-waves scatter and wheel from the
        works beyond;
The air is dark with north and with sulphur, the grass is a darker green,
And people darkly invested with purple move palpable through the
        scene.

Soundlessly down across the counties, out of the resonant gloom
That wraps the north in stupor and purple travels the deep, slow boom
Of the man-life north-imprisoned, shut in the hum of the purpled steel
As it spins to sleep on its motion, drugged dense in the sleep of the
        wheel.

Out of the sleep, from the gloom of motion, soundlessly, somnambule
Moans and booms the soul of a people imprisoned, asleep in the rule
Of the strong machine that runs mesmeric, booming the spell of its
        word
Upon them and moving them helpless, mechanic, their will to its will
        deferred.

Yet all the while comes the droning inaudible, out of the violet air,
The moaning of sleep-bound beings in travail that toil and are will-less
        there
In the spell-bound north, convulsive now with a dream near morning,
        strong
With violent achings heaving to burst the sleep that is now not long.

BITTERNESS OF DEATH

I

Ah, stern, cold man,
How can you lie so relentless hard
While I wash you with weeping water!
Do you set your face against the daughter
Of life? Can you never discard
Your curt pride's ban?

You masquerader!
How can you shame to act this part
Of unswerving indifference to me?
You want at last, ah me!
To break my heart
Evader!

You know your mouth
Was always sooner to soften
Even than your eyes.
Now shut it lies
Relentless, however often
I kiss it in drouth.

It has no breath
Nor any relaxing. Where,
Where are you, what have you done?
What is this mouth of stone?
How did you dare
Take cover in death!

II

Once you could see,
The white moon show like a breast revealed
By the slipping shawl of stars.
Could see the small stars tremble
As the heart beneath did wield
Systole, diastole.

All the lovely macrocosm
Was woman once to you,
Bride to your groom.
No tree in bloom
But it leaned you a new
White bosom.

And always and ever
Soft as a summering tree
Unfolds from the sky, for your good,
Unfolded womanhood;
Shedding you down as a tree
Sheds its flowers on a river.

I saw your brows
Set like rocks beside a sea of gloom,
And I shed my very soul down into your thought;
Like flowers I fell, to be caught
On the comforted pool, like bloom
That leaves the boughs.

III

Oh, masquerader,
With a hard face white-enamelled,
What are you now?
Do you care no longer how
My heart is trammelled,
Evader?

Is this you, after all,
Metallic, obdurate
With bowels of steel?
Did you *never* feel?—
Cold, insensate,
Mechanical!

Ah, no!—you multiform,
You that I loved, you wonderful,
You who darkened and shone,
You were many men in one;
But never this null
This never-warm!

Is this the sum of you?
Is it all nought?
Cold, metal-cold?
Are you all told
Here, iron-wrought?
Is *this* what's become of you?

SEVEN SEALS

Since this is the last night I keep you home,
Come, I will consecrate you for the journey.

Rather I had you would not go. Nay come,
I will not again reproach you. Lie back
And let me love you a long time ere you go.
For you are sullen-hearted still, and lack
The will to love me. But even so
I will set a seal upon you from my lip,
Will set a guard of honour at each door,
Seal up each channel out of which might slip
Your love for me.

           I kiss your mouth. Ah, love,
Could I but seal its ruddy, shining spring
Of passion, parch it up, destroy, remove
Its softly-stirring crimson welling-up
Of kisses! Oh, help me, God! Here at the source
I'd lie for ever drinking and drawing in
Your fountains, as heaven drinks from out their course
The floods.

I close your ears with kisses
And seal your nostrils; and round your neck you'll wear—
Nay, let me work—a delicate chain of kisses.
Like beads they go around, and not one misses
To touch its fellow on either side.

                  And there
Full mid-between the champaign of your breast
I place a great and burning seal of love
Like a dark rose, a mystery of rest
On the slow bubbling of your rhythmic heart.

Nay, I persist, and very faith shall keep
You integral to me. Each door, each mystic port
Of egress from you I will seal and steep
In perfect chrism.
              Now it is done. The mort
Will sound in heaven before it is undone.

But let me finish what I have begun
And shirt you now invulnerable in the mail
Of iron kisses, kisses linked like steel.
Put greaves upon your thighs and knees, and frail
Webbing of steel on your feet. So you shall feel
Ensheathed invulnerable with me, with seven
Great seals upon your outgoings, and woven
Chain of my mystic will wrapped perfectly
Upon you, wrapped in indomitable me.

READING A LETTER

She sits on the recreation ground
  Under an oak whose yellow buds dot the pale blue sky.
The young grass twinkles in the wind, and the sound
  Of the wind in the knotted buds in a canopy.

So sitting under the knotted canopy
  Of the wind, she is lifted and carried away as in a balloon
Across the insensible void, till she stoops to see
  The sandy desert beneath her, the dreary platoon.

She knows the waste all dry beneath her, in one place
  Stirring with earth-coloured life, ever turning and stirring.
But never the motion has a human face
  Nor sound, save intermittent machinery whirring.

And so again, on the recreation ground
  She alights a stranger, wondering, unused to the scene;
Suffering at sight of the children playing around,
  Hurt at the chalk-coloured tulips, and the evening-green.

TWENTY YEARS AGO

Round the house were lilacs and strawberries
  And foal-foots spangling the paths,
And far away on the sand-hills, dewberries
  Caught dust from the sea's long swaths.

Up the wolds the woods were walking,
  And nuts fell out of their hair.
At the gate the nets hung, balking
  The star-lit rush of a hare.

In the autumn fields, the stubble
  Tinkled the music of gleaning.
At a mother's knees, the trouble
  Lost all its meaning.

Yea, what good beginnings
  To this sad end!
Have we had our innings?
  God forfend!

INTIME

Returning, I find her just the same,
At just the same old delicate game.

Still she says: "Nay, loose no flame
To lick me up and do me harm!
Be all yourself!—for oh, the charm
Of your heart of fire in which I look!
Oh, better there than in any book
Glow and enact the dramas and dreams
I love for ever!—there it seems
You are lovelier than life itself, till desire
Comes licking through the bars of your lips
And over my face the stray fire slips,
Leaving a burn and an ugly smart
That will have the oil of illusion. Oh, heart
Of fire and beauty, loose no more
Your reptile flames of lust; ah, store
Your passion in the basket of your soul,
Be all yourself, one bonny, burning coal
That stays with steady joy of its own fire.
But do not seek to take me by desire.
Oh, do not seek to thrust on me your fire!
For in the firing all my porcelain
Of flesh does crackle and shiver and break in pain,
My ivory and marble black with stain,
My veil of sensitive mystery rent in twain,
My altars sullied, I, bereft, remain
A priestess execrable, taken in vain—"

                 So the refrain
Sings itself over, and so the game
Re-starts itself wherein I am kept
Like a glowing brazier faintly blue of flame
So that the delicate love-adept
Can warm her hands and invite her soul,
Sprinkling incense and salt of words
And kisses pale, and sipping the toll
Of incense-smoke that rises like birds.

Yet I've forgotten in playing this game,
Things I have known that shall have no name;
Forgetting the place from which I came
I watch her ward away the flame,
Yet warm herself at the fire—then blame
Me that I flicker in the basket;
Me that I glow not with content
To have my substance so subtly spent;
Me that I interrupt her game.
I ought to be proud that she should ask it
Of me to be her fire-opal—.

It is well
Since I am here for so short a spell
Not to interrupt her?—Why should I
Break in by making any reply!

TWO WIVES

I

Into the shadow-white chamber silts the white
Flux of another dawn. The wind that all night
Long has waited restless, suddenly wafts
A whirl like snow from the plum-trees and the pear,
Till petals heaped between the window-shafts
       In a drift die there.

A nurse in white, at the dawning, flower-foamed pane
Draws down the blinds, whose shadows scarcely stain
The white rugs on the floor, nor the silent bed
That rides the room like a frozen berg, its crest
Finally ridged with the austere line of the dead
       Stretched out at rest.

Less than a year the fourfold feet had pressed
The peaceful floor, when fell the sword on their rest.
Yet soon, too soon, she had him home again
With wounds between them, and suffering like a guest
That will not go. Now suddenly going, the pain
       Leaves an empty breast.

II

A tall woman, with her long white gown aflow
As she strode her limbs amongst it, once more
She hastened towards the room. Did she know
As she listened in silence outside the silent door?
Entering, she saw him in outline, raised on a pyre
       Awaiting the fire.

Upraised on the bed, with feet erect as a bow,
Like the prow of a boat, his head laid back like the stern
Of a ship that stands in a shadowy sea of snow
With frozen rigging, she saw him; she drooped like a fern
Refolding, she slipped to the floor as a ghost-white peony slips
       When the thread clips.

180

Soft she lay as a shed flower fallen, nor heard
The ominous entry, nor saw the other love,
The dark, the grave-eyed mistress who thus dared
At such an hour to lay her claim, above
A stricken wife, so sunk in oblivion, bowed
                With misery, no more proud.

III

The stranger's hair was shorn like a lad's dark poll
And pale her ivory face: her eyes would fail
In silence when she looked: for all the whole
Darkness of failure was in them, without avail.
Dark in indomitable failure, she who had lost
                Now claimed the host,

She softly passed the sorrowful flower shed
In blonde and white on the floor, nor even turned
Her head aside, but straight towards the bed
Moved with slow feet, and her eyes' flame steadily burned.
She looked at him as he lay with banded cheek,
                And she started to speak

Softly: "I knew it would come to this," she said,
"I knew that some day, soon, I should find you thus.
So I did not fight you. You went your way instead
Of coming mine—and of the two of us
I died the first, I, in the after-life
                Am now your wife."

IV

"'Twas I whose fingers did draw up the young
Plant of your body: to me you looked e'er sprung
The secret of the moon within your eyes!
My mouth you met before your fine red mouth
Was set to song—and never your song denies
                My love, till you went south."

"'Twas I who placed the bloom of manhood on
Your youthful smoothness: I fleeced where fleece was none
Your fervent limbs with flickers and tendrils of new
Knowledge; I set your heart to its stronger beat;
I put my strength upon you, and I threw
                My life at your feet."

"But I whom the years had reared to be your bride,
Who for years was sun for your shivering, shade for your sweat,
Who for one strange year was as a bride to you—you set me aside
With all the old, sweet things of our youth;—and never yet
Have I ceased to grieve that I was not great enough
        To defeat your baser stuff."

V

"But you are given back again to me
Who have kept intact for you your virginity.
Who for the rest of life walk out of care,
Indifferent here of myself, since I am gone
Where you are gone, and you and I out there
        Walk now as one."

"Your widow am I, and only I. I dream
God bows his head and grants me this supreme
Pure look of your last dead face, whence now is gone
The mobility, the panther's gambolling,
And all your being is given to me, so none
        Can mock my struggling."

"And now at last I kiss your perfect face,
Perfecting now our unfinished, first embrace.
Your young hushed look that then saw God ablaze
In every bush, is given you back, and we
Are met at length to finish our rest of days
        In a unity."

HEIMWEH

Far-off the lily-statues stand white-ranked in the garden at home.
Would God they were shattered quickly, the cattle would tread them
        out in the loam.
I wish the elder trees in flower could suddenly heave, and burst
The walls of the house, and nettles puff out from the hearth at which I
        was nursed.

It stands so still in the hush composed of trees and inviolate peace,
The home of my fathers, the place that is mine, my fate and my old
        increase.
And now that the skies are falling, the world is spouting in fountains of
        dirt,
I would give my soul for the homestead to fall with me, go with me,
        both in one hurt.

DÉBÂCLE

The trees in trouble because of autumn,
  And scarlet berries falling from the bush,
And all the myriad houseless seeds
  Loosing hold in the wind's insistent push

Moan softly with autumnal parturition,
  Poor, obscure fruits extruded out of light
Into the world of shadow, carried down
  Between the bitter knees of the after-night.

Bushed in an uncouth ardour, coiled at core
  With a knot of life that only bliss can unravel,
Fall all the fruits most bitterly into earth
  Bitterly into corrosion bitterly travel.

What is it internecine that is locked,
  By very fierceness into a quiescence
Within the rage? We shall not know till it burst
  Out of corrosion into new florescence.

Nay, but how tortured is the frightful seed
  The spark intense within it, all without
Mordant corrosion gnashing and champing hard
  For ruin on the naked small redoubt.

Bitter, to fold the issue, and make no sally;
  To have the mystery, but not go forth;
To bear, but retaliate nothing, given to save
  The spark in storms of corrosion, as seeds from the north.

The sharper, more horrid the pressure, the harder the heart
  That saves the blue grain of eternal fire
Within its quick, committed to hold and wait
  And suffer unheeding, only forbidden to expire.

NARCISSUS

Where the minnows trace
A glinting web quick hid in the gloom of the brook,
When I think of the place
And remember the small lad lying intent to look
Through the shadowy face
At the little fish thread-threading the watery nook—

It seems to me
The woman you are should be nixie, there is a pool
Where we ought to be.
You undine-clear and pearly, soullessly cool
And waterly
The pool for my limbs to fathom, my soul's last school.

Narcissus
Ventured so long ago in the deeps of reflection.
Illyssus
Broke the bounds and beyond!—Dim recollection
Of fishes
Soundlessly moving in heaven's other direction!

Be
Undine towards the waters, moving back;
For me
A pool! Put off the soul you've got, oh lack
Your human self immortal; take the watery track.

AUTUMN SUNSHINE

The sun sets out the autumn crocuses
And fills them up a pouring measure
Of death-producing wine, till treasure
Runs waste down their chalices.

All, all Persephone's pale cups of mould
Are on the board, are over-filled;
The portion to the gods is spilled;
Now, mortals all, take hold!

The time is now, the wine-cup full and full
Of lambent heaven, a pledging-cup;
Let now all mortal men take up
The drink, and a long, strong pull.

Out of the hell-queen's cup, the heaven's pale wine—
Drink then, invisible heroes, drink.
Lips to the vessels, never shrink,
Throats to the heavens incline.

And take within the wine the god's great oath
By heaven and earth and hellish stream
To break this sick and nauseous dream
We writhe and lust in, both.

Swear, in the pale wine poured from the cups of the queen
  Of hell, to wake and be free
  From this nightmare we writhe in,
Break out of this foul has-been.

ON THAT DAY

  On that day
I shall put roses on roses, and cover your grave
With multitude of white roses: and since you were brave
  One bright red ray.

  So people, passing under
The ash-trees of the valley-road, will raise
Their eyes and look at the grave on the hill, in wonder,
  Wondering mount, and put the flowers asunder

  To see whose praise
Is blazoned here so white and so bloodily red.
Then they will say: "'Tis long since she is dead,
  Who has remembered her after many days?"

  And standing there
They will consider how you went your ways
Unnoticed among them, a still queen lost in the maze
  Of this earthly affair.

  A queen, they'll say,
Has slept unnoticed on a forgotten hill.
Sleeps on unknown, unnoticed there, until
  Dawns my insurgent day.

BAY .. A BOOK OF .. POEMS (1919)

GUARDS!

A Review in Hyde Park 1913. The Crowd Watches.

Where the trees rise like cliffs, proud and blue-tinted in the distance,
Between the cliffs of the trees, on the grey-green park
Rests a still line of soldiers, red motionless range of guards
Smouldering with darkened busbies beneath the bayonets' slant rain.

Colossal in nearness a blue police sits still on his horse
Guarding the path; his hand relaxed at his thigh,
And skyward his face is immobile, eyelids aslant
In tedium, and mouth relaxed as if smiling—ineffable tedium!

So! So! Gaily a general canters across the space,
With white plumes blinking under the evening grey sky.
And suddenly, as if the ground moved
The red range heaves in slow, magnetic reply.

EVOLUTIONS OF SOLDIERS

The red range heaves and compulsory sways, ah see! in the flush of a
    march
Softly-impulsive advancing as water towards a weir from the arch
Of shadow emerging as blood emerges from inward shades of our night
Encroaching towards a crisis, a meeting, a spasm and throb of delight.

The wave of soldiers, the coming wave, the throbbing red breast of
    approach
Upon us; dark eyes as here beneath the busbies glittering, dark threats
    that broach
Our beached vessel; darkened rencontre inhuman, and closed warm
    lips, and dark
Mouth-hair of soldiers passing above us, over the wreck of our bark.

And so, it is ebb-time, they turn, the eyes beneath the busbies are gone.
But the blood has suspended its timbre, the heart from out of oblivion
Knows but the retreat of the burning shoulders, the red-swift waves of
    the sweet
Fire horizontal declining and ebbing, the twilit ebb of retreat.

THE LITTLE TOWN AT EVENING

The chime of the bells, and the church clock striking eight
Solemnly and distinctly cries down the babel of children still playing in
        the hay.
The church draws nearer upon us, gentle and great
In shadow, covering us up with her grey.

Like drowsy children the houses fall asleep
Under the fleece of shadow, as in between
Tall and dark the church moves, anxious to keep
Their sleeping, cover them soft unseen.

Hardly a murmur comes from the sleeping brood,
I wish the church had covered me up with the rest
In the home-place. Why is it she should exclude
Me so distinctly from sleeping with those I love best?

LAST HOURS

The cool of an oak's unchequered shade
Falls on me as I lie in deep grass
Which rushes upward, blade beyond blade,
While higher the darting grass-flowers pass
Piercing the blue with their crocketed spires
And waving flags, and the ragged fires
Of the sorrel's cresset—a green, brave town
Vegetable, new in renown.

Over the tree's edge, as over a mountain
Surges the white of the moon,
A cloud comes up like the surge of a fountain,
Pressing round and low at first, but soon
Heaving and piling a round white dome.
How lovely it is to be at home
Like an insect in the grass
Letting life pass.

There's a scent of clover crept through my hair
From the full resource of some purple dome
Where that lumbering bee, who can hardly bear
His burden above me, never has clomb.
But not even the scent of insouciant flowers
Makes pause the hours.

Down the valley roars a townward train.
I hear it through the grass
Dragging the links of my shortening chain
Southwards, alas!

TOWN IN 1917

London
Used to wear her lights splendidly,
Flinging her shawl-fringe over the River,
Tassels in abandon.

And up in the sky
A two-eyed clock, like an owl
Solemnly used to approve, chime, chiming,
Approval, goggle-eyed fowl.

There are no gleams on the River,
No goggling clock;
No sound from St. Stephen's;
No lamp-fringed frock.

Instead,
Darkness, and skin-wrapped
Fleet, hurrying limbs,
Soft-footed dead.

London
Original, wolf-wrapped
In pelts of wolves, all her luminous
Garments gone.

London, with hair
Like a forest darkness, like a marsh
Of rushes, ere the Romans
Broke in her lair.

It is well
That London, lair of sudden
Male and female darknesses
Has broken her spell.

AFTER THE OPERA

Down the stone stairs
Girls with their large eyes wide with tragedy
Lift looks of shocked and momentous emotion up at me.
And I smile.

Ladies
Stepping like birds with their bright and pointed feet
Peer anxiously forth, as if for a boat to carry them out of the wreckage,
And among the wreck of the theatre crowd
I stand and smile.

They take tragedy so becomingly.
Which pleases me.

But when I meet the weary eyes
The reddened aching eyes of the bar-man with thin arms,
I am glad to go back to where I came from.

GOING BACK

The Night turns slowly round,
Swift trains go by in a rush of light;
Slow trains steal past.
This train beats anxiously, outward bound.

But I am not here.
I am away, beyond the scope of this turning;
There, where the pivot is, the axis
Of all this gear.

I, who sit in tears,
I, whose heart is torn with parting;
Who cannot bear to think back to the departure platform;
My spirit hears

Voices of men
Sound of artillery, aeroplanes, presences,
And more than all, the dead-sure silence,
The pivot again.

There, at the axis
Pain, or love, or grief
Sleep on speed; in dead certainty;
Pure relief.

There, at the pivot
Time sleeps again.
No has-been, no here-after; only the perfected
Silence of men.

ON THE MARCH

We are out on the open road.
Through the low west window a cold light flows
On the floor where never my numb feet trode
Before; onward the strange road goes.

Soon the spaces of the western sky
With shutters of sombre cloud will close.
But we'll still be together, this road and I,
Together, wherever the long road goes.

The wind chases by us, and over the corn
Pale shadows flee from us as if from their foes.
Like a snake we thresh on the long, forlorn
Land, as onward the long road goes.

From the sky, the low, tired moon fades out;
Through the poplars the night-wind blows;
Pale, sleepy phantoms are tossed about
As the wind asks whither the wan road goes.

Away in the distance wakes a lamp.
Inscrutable small lights glitter in rows.
But they come no nearer, and still we tramp
Onward, wherever the strange road goes.

Beat after beat falls sombre and dull.
The wind is unchanging, not one of us knows
What will be in the final lull
When we find the place where this dead road goes.

For something must come, since we pass and pass
Along in the coiled, convulsive throes
Of this marching, along with the invisible grass
That goes wherever this old road goes.

Perhaps we shall come to oblivion.
Perhaps we shall march till our tired toes
Tread over the edge of the pit, and we're gone
Down the endless slope where the last road goes.

If so, let us forge ahead, straight on
If we're going to sleep the sleep with those
That fall forever, knowing none
Of this land whereon the wrong road goes.

BOMBARDMENT

The Town has opened to the sun.
Like a flat red lily with a million petals
She unfolds, she comes undone.

A sharp sky brushes upon
The myriad glittering chimney-tips
As she gently exhales to the sun.

Hurrying creatures run
Down the labyrinth of the sinister flower.
What is it they shun?

A dark bird falls from the sun.
It curves in a rush to the heart of the vast
Flower: the day has begun.

WINTER-LULL

Because of the silent snow, we are all hushed
    Into awe.
No sound of guns, nor overhead no rushed
    Vibration to draw
Our attention out of the void wherein we are crushed.

A crow floats past on level wings
    Noiselessly.
Uninterrupted silence swings
    Invisibly, inaudibly
To and fro in our misgivings.

We do not look at each other, we hide
    Our daunted eyes.
White earth, and ruins, ourselves, and nothing beside.
    It all belies
Our existence; we wait, and are still denied.

We are folded together, men and the snowy ground
    Into nullity.
There is silence, only the silence, never a sound
    Nor a verity
To assist us; disastrously silence-bound!

THE ATTACK

When we came out of the wood
Was a great light!
The night uprisen stood
In white.

I wondered, I looked around
It was so fair. The bright
Stubble upon the ground
Shone white

Like any field of snow;
Yet warm the chase
Of faint night-breaths did go
Across my face!

White-bodied and warm the night was,
Sweet-scented to hold in my throat.
White and alight the night was.
A pale stroke smote

The pulse through the whole bland being
Which was This and me;
A pulse that still went fleeing,
Yet did not flee.

After the terrible rage, the death,
This wonder stood glistening?
All shapes of wonder, with suspended breath,
Arrested listening

In ecstatic reverie.
The whole, white Night!—
With wonder, every black tree
Blossomed outright.

I saw the transfiguration
And the present Host.
Transubstantiation
Of the Luminous Ghost.

OBSEQUIAL ODE

Surely you've trodden straight
    To the very door!
Surely you took your fate
Faultlessly. Now it's too late
    To say more.

    It is evident you were right,
    That man has a course to go
A voyage to sail beyond the charted seas.
You have passed from out of sight
    And my questions blow
Back from the straight horizon that ends all one sees.

    Now like a vessel in port
    You unlade your riches unto death,
And glad are the eager dead to receive you there.
    Let the dead sort
Your cargo out, breath from breath
Let them disencumber your bounty, let them all share.

    I imagine dead hands are brighter,
    Their fingers in sunset shine
With jewels of passion once broken through you as a prism
Breaks light into jewels; and dead breasts whiter
    For your wrath; and yes, I opine
They anoint their brows with your blood, as a perfect chrism.

    On your body, the beaten anvil,
    Was hammered out
That moon-like sword the ascendant dead unsheathe
Against us; sword that no man will
    Put to rout;
Sword that severs the question from us who breathe.

Surely you've trodden straight
    To the very door.
You have surely achieved your fate;
And the perfect dead are elate
    To have won once more.

Now to the dead you are giving
    Your last allegiance.
But what of us who are living
And fearful yet of believing
    In your pitiless legions.

SHADES

Shall I tell you, then, how it is?—
There came a cloven gleam
Like a tongue of darkened flame
To flicker in me.

And so I seem
To have you still the same
In one world with me.

In the flicker of a flower,
In a worm that is blind, yet strives,
In a mouse that pauses to listen

Glimmers our
Shadow; yet it deprives
Them none of their glisten.

In every shaken morsel
I see our shadow tremble
As if it rippled from out of us hand in hand.

As if it were part and parcel,
One shadow, and we need not dissemble
Our darkness: do you understand?

For I have told you plainly how it is.

BREAD UPON THE WATERS

So you are lost to me!
Ah you, you ear of corn straight lying,
What food is this for the darkly flying
Fowls of the Afterwards!

White bread afloat on the waters,
Cast out by the hand that scatters
Food untowards,

Will you come back when the tide turns?
After many days? My heart yearns
To know.

Will you return after many days
To say your say as a traveller says,
More marvel than woe?

Drift then, for the sightless birds
And the fish in shadow-waved herds
To approach you.

Drift then, bread cast out;
Drift, lest I fall in doubt,
And reproach you.

For you are lost to me!

RUINATION

The sun is bleeding its fires upon the mist
That huddles in grey heaps coiling and holding back.
Like cliffs abutting in shadow a drear grey sea
Some street-ends thrust forward their stack.

On the misty waste-lands, away from the flushing grey
Of the morning the elms are loftily dimmed, and tall
As if moving in air towards us, tall angels
Of darkness advancing steadily over us all.

RONDEAU OF A CONSCIENTIOUS OBJECTOR

The hours have tumbled their leaden, monotonous sands
And piled them up in a dull grey heap in the West.
I carry my patience sullenly through the waste lands;
To-morrow will pour them all back, the dull hours I detest.

I force my cart through the sodden filth that is pressed
Into ooze, and the sombre dirt spouts up at my hands
As I make my way in twilight now to rest.
The hours have tumbled their leaden, monotonous sands.

A twisted thorn-tree still in the evening stands
Defending the memory of leaves and the happy round nest.
But mud has flooded the homes of these weary lands
And piled them up in a dull grey heap in the West.

All day has the clank of iron on iron distressed
The nerve-bare place. Now a little silence expands
And a gasp of relief. But the soul is still compressed:
I carry my patience sullenly through the waste lands.

The hours have ceased to fall, and a star commands
Shadows to cover our stricken manhood, and blest
Sleep to make us forget: but he understands:
To-morrow will pour them all back, the dull hours
I detest.

TOMMIES IN THE TRAIN

The Sun Shines,
The coltsfoot flowers along the railway banks
Shine like flat coin which Jove in thanks
Strews each side the lines.

A steeple
In purple elms, daffodils
Sparkle beneath; luminous hills
Beyond—and no people.

England, Oh Danaë
To this spring of cosmic gold
That falls on your lap of mould!
What then are we?

What are we
Clay-coloured, who roll in fatigue
As the train falls league by league
From our destiny?

A hand is over my face,
A cold hand. I peep between the fingers
To watch the world that lingers
Behind, yet keeps pace.

Always there, as I peep
Between the fingers that cover my face!
Which then is it that falls from its place
And rolls down the steep?

Is it the train
That falls like meteorite
Backward into space, to alight
Never again?

Or is it the illusory world
That falls from reality
As we look? Or are we
Like a thunderbolt hurled?

One or another
Is lost, since we fall apart
Endlessly, in one motion depart
From each other.

WAR-BABY

The Child like mustard-seed
Rolls out of the husk of death
    Into the woman's fertile, fathomless lap.

Look, it has taken root!
See how it flourisheth.
    See how it rises with magical, rosy sap!

As for our faith, it was there
When we did not know, did not care;
    It fell from our husk like a little, hasty seed.

Sing, it is all we need.
Sing, for the little weed
    Will flourish its branches in heaven when we slumber beneath.

NOSTALGIA

The waning moon looks upward; this grey night
Slopes round the heavens in one smooth curve
Of easy sailing; odd red wicks serve
To show where the ships at sea move out of sight.

The place is palpable me, for here I was born
Of this self-same darkness. Yet the shadowy house below
Is out of bounds, and only the old ghosts know
I have come, I feel them whimper in welcome, and mourn.

My father suddenly died in the harvesting corn
And the place is no longer ours. Watching, I hear
No sound from the strangers, the place is dark, and fear
Opens my eyes till the roots of my vision seems torn.

Can I go no nearer, never towards the door?
The ghosts and I we mourn together, and shrink
In the shadow of the cart-shed. Must we hover on the brink
Forever, and never enter the homestead any more?

Is it irrevocable? Can I really not go
Through the open yard-way? Can I not go past the sheds
And through to the mowie?—Only the dead in their beds
Can know the fearful anguish that this is so.

I kiss the stones, I kiss the moss on the wall,
And wish I could pass impregnate into the place.
I wish I could take it all in a last embrace.
I wish with my breast I here could annihilate it all.

TORTOISES (1921)

BABY TORTOISE

You know what it is to be born alone,
Baby tortoise!

The first day to heave your feet little by little from the shell,
Not yet awake,
And remain lapsed on earth,
Not quite alive.

A tiny, fragile, half-animate bean.

To open your tiny beak-mouth, that looks as if it would never open,
Like some iron door;
To lift the upper hawk-beak from the lower base
And reach your skinny little neck
And take your first bite at some dim bit of herbage,
Alone, small insect,
Tiny bright-eye,
Slow one.

To take your first solitary bite
And move on your slow, solitary hunt.
Your bright, dark little eye,
Your eye of a dark disturbed night,
Under its slow lid, tiny baby tortoise,
So indomitable.

No one ever heard you complain.

You draw your head forward, slowly, from your little wimple
And set forward, slow-dragging, on your four-pinned toes,
Rowing slowly forward.
Whither away, small bird?

Rather like a baby working its limbs,
Except that you make slow, ageless progress
And a baby makes none.

The touch of sun excites you,
And the long ages, and the lingering chill
Make you pause to yawn,
Opening your impervious mouth,
Suddenly beak-shaped, and very wide, like some suddenly gaping
        pincers;
Soft red tongue, and hard thin gums,
Then close the wedge of your little mountain front,
Your face, baby tortoise.

Do you wonder at the world, as slowly you turn your head in its
        wimple
And look with laconic, black eyes?
Or is sleep coming over you again,
The non-life?

You are so hard to wake.

Are you able to wonder?

Or is it just your indomitable will and pride of the first life
Looking round
And slowly pitching itself against the inertia
Which had seemed invincible?

The vast inanimate,
And the fine brilliance of your so tiny eye.
Challenger.

Nay, tiny shell-bird,
What a huge vast inanimate it is, that you must row against,
What an incalculable inertia.

Challenger.
Little Ulysses, fore-runner,
No bigger than my thumb-nail,
Buon viaggio.

All animate creation on your shoulder,
Set forth, little Titan, under your battle-shield.

The ponderous, preponderate,
Inanimate universe;
And you are slowly moving, pioneer, you alone.

How vivid your travelling seems now, in the troubled sunshine,
Stoic, Ulyssean atom;
Suddenly hasty, reckless, on high toes.

Voiceless little bird,
Resting your head half out of your wimple
In the slow dignity of your eternal pause.
Alone, with no sense of being alone,
And hence six times more solitary;
Fulfilled of the slow passion of pitching through immemorial ages
Your little round house in the midst of chaos.

Over the garden earth,
Small bird,
Over the edge of all things.

Traveller,
With your tail tucked a little on one side
Like a gentleman in a long-skirted coat.

All life carried on your shoulder,
Invincible fore-runner.

TORTOISE-SHELL

The Cross, the Cross
Goes deeper in than we know,
Deeper into life;
Right into the marrow
And through the bone.

Along the back of the baby tortoise
The scales are locked in an arch like a bridge,
Scale-lapping, like a lobster's sections
Or a bee's.

Then crossways down his sides
Tiger-stripes and wasp-bands.
Five, and five again, and five again,
And round the edges twenty-five little ones,
The sections of the baby tortoise shell.

Four, and a keystone;
Four, and a keystone;
Four, and a keystone;
Then twenty-four, and a tiny little keystone.

It needed Pythagoras to see life placing her counters on the living back
Of the baby tortoise;
Life establishing the first eternal mathematical tablet,
Not in stone, like the Judean Lord, or bronze, but in life-clouded, life-
    rosy tortoise-shell.

The first little mathematical gentleman
Stepping, wee mite, in his loose trousers
Under all the eternal dome of mathematical law.

Fives, and tens,
Threes and fours and twelves,
All the volte face of decimals,
The whirligig of dozens and the pinnacle of seven,

Turn him on his back,
The kicking little beetle,
And there again, on his shell-tender, earth-touching belly,
The long cleavage of division, upright of the eternal cross.

And on either side count five,
On each side, two above, on each side, two below
The dark bar horizontal.

The Cross!
It goes right through him, the sprottling insect,
Through his cross-wise cloven psyche,
Through his five-fold complex-nature.

So turn him over on his toes again;
Four pin-point toes, and a problematical thumb-piece,
Four rowing limbs, and one wedge-balancing-head,
Four and one makes five, which is the clue to all mathematics.

The Lord wrote it all down on the little slate
Of the baby tortoise.
Outward and visible indication of the plan within,
The complex, manifold involvedness of an individual creature
Blotted out
On this small bird, this rudiment,
This little dome, this pediment
Of all creation,
This slow one.

TORTOISE FAMILY CONNECTIONS

On he goes, the little one,
Bud of the universe,
Pediment of life.

Setting off somewhere, apparently.
Whither away, brisk egg?

His mother deposited him on the soil as if he were no more than
    droppings,
And now he scuffles tinily past her as if she were an old rusty tin.

A mere obstacle,
He veers round the slow great mound of her.
Tortoises always foresee obstacles.

It is no use my saying to him in an emotional voice:
"This is your Mother, she laid you when you were an egg."

He does not even trouble to answer: "Woman, what have I to do with
    thee?"
He wearily looks the other way,
And she even more wearily looks another way still,
Each with the utmost apathy,
Incognizant,
Unaware,
Nothing.

As for papa,
He snaps when I offer him his offspring,
Just as he snaps when I poke a bit of stick at him,
Because he is irascible this morning, an irascible tortoise
Being touched with love, and devoid of fatherliness.

Father and mother,
And three little brothers,
And all rambling aimless, like little perambulating pebbles scattered in
    the garden,
Not knowing each other from bits of earth or old tins.

Except that papa and mama are old acquaintances, of course,
But family feeling there is none, not even the beginnings.

Fatherless, motherless, brotherless, sisterless
Little tortoise.

Row on then, small pebble,
Over the clods of the autumn, wind-chilled sunshine,
Young gayety.

Does he look for a companion?

No, no, don't think it.
He doesn't know he is alone;
Isolation is his birthright,
This atom.

To row forward, and reach himself tall on spiny toes,
To travel, to burrow into a little loose earth, afraid of the night,
To crop a little substance,
To move, and to be quite sure that he is moving:
Basta!

To be a tortoise!
Think of it, in a garden of inert clods
A brisk, brindled little tortoise, all to himself—
Croesus!

In a garden of pebbles and insects
To roam, and feel the slow heart beat
Tortoise-wise, the first bell sounding
From the warm blood, in the dark-creation morning.

Moving, and being himself,
Slow, and unquestioned,
And inordinately there, O stoic!
Wandering in the slow triumph of his own existence,
Ringing the soundless bell of his presence in chaos,
And biting the frail grass arrogantly,
Decidedly arrogantly.

LUI ET ELLE

She is large and matronly
And rather dirty,
A little sardonic-looking, as if domesticity had driven her to it.

Though what she does, except lay four eggs at random in the garden
          once a year
And put up with her husband,
I don't know.

She likes to eat.
She hurries up, striding reared on long uncanny legs,
When food is going.
Oh yes, she can make haste when she likes.

She snaps the soft bread from my hand in great mouthfuls,
Opening her rather pretty wedge of an iron, pristine face
Into an enormously wide-beaked mouth
Like sudden curved scissors,
And gulping at more than she can swallow, and working her thick, soft
        tongue,
And having the bread hanging over her chin.

O Mistress, Mistress,
Reptile mistress,
Your eye is very dark, very bright,
And it never softens
Although you watch.

She knows,
She knows well enough to come for food,
Yet she sees me not;
Her bright eye sees, but not me, not anything,
Sightful, sightless, seeing and visionless,
Reptile mistress.

Taking bread in her curved, gaping, toothless mouth,
She has no qualm when she catches my finger in her steel overlapping
        gums,
But she hangs on, and my shout and my shrinking are nothing to her,
She does not even know she is nipping me with her curved beak.
Snake-like she draws at my finger, while I drag it in horror away.

Mistress, reptile mistress,
You are almost too large, I am almost frightened.

He is much smaller,
Dapper beside her,
And ridiculously small.

Her laconic eye has an earthy, materialistic look,
His, poor darling, is almost fiery.

His wimple, his blunt-prowed face,
His low forehead, his skinny neck, his long, scaled, striving legs,
So striving, striving,
Are all more delicate than she,
And he has a cruel scar on his shell.

Poor darling, biting at her feet,
Running beside her like a dog, biting her earthy, splay feet,
Nipping her ankles,
Which she drags apathetic away, though without retreating into her
        shell.

Agelessly silent,
And with a grim, reptile determination,
Cold, voiceless age-after-age behind him, serpents' long obstinacy
Of horizontal persistence.

Little old man
Scuffling beside her, bending down, catching his opportunity,
Parting his steel-trap face, so suddenly, and seizing her scaly ankle,
And hanging grimly on,
Letting go at last as she drags away,
And closing his steel-trap face.

His steel-trap, stoic, ageless, handsome face.
Alas, what a fool he looks in this scuffle.

And how he feels it!
The lonely rambler, the stoic, dignified stalker through chaos,
The immune, the animate,
Enveloped in isolation,
Forerunner.
Now look at him!

Alas, the spear is through the side of his isolation.
His adolescence saw him crucified into sex,
Doomed, in the long crucifixion of desire, to seek his consummation
        beyond himself.
Divided into passionate duality,
He, so finished and immune, now broken into desirous fragmentariness,
Doomed to make an intolerable fool of himself
In his effort toward completion again.

Poor little earthy house-inhabiting Osiris,
The mysterious bull tore him at adolescence into pieces,
And he must struggle after reconstruction, ignominiously.

And so behold him following the tail
Of that mud-hovel of his slowly-rambling spouse,
Like some unhappy bull at the tail of a cow,
But with more than bovine, grim, earth-dank persistence,
Suddenly seizing the ugly ankle as she stretches out to walk,
Roaming over the sods,
Or, if it happen to show, at her pointed, heavy tail
Beneath the low-dropping back-board of her shell.

Their two shells like doomed boats bumping,
Hers huge, his small;
Their splay feet rambling and rowing like paddles,
And stumbling mixed up in one another,
In the race of love—
Two tortoises,
She huge, he small.

She seems earthily apathetic,
And he has a reptile's awful persistence.

I heard a woman pitying her, pitying the Mère Tortue.
While I, I pity Monsieur.
"He pesters her and torments her," said the woman.
How much more is *he* pestered and tormented, say I.

What can he do?
He is dumb, he is visionless,
Conceptionless.
His black, sad-lidded eye sees but beholds not
As her earthen mound moves on,
But he catches the folds of vulnerable, leathery skin,
Nail-studded, that shake beneath her shell,
And drags at these with his beak,
Drags and drags and bites,
While she pulls herself free, and rows her dull mound along.

TORTOISE GALLANTRY

Making his advances
He does not look at her, nor sniff at her,
No, not even sniff at her, his nose is blank.

Only he senses the vulnerable folds of skin
That work beneath her while she sprawls along
In her ungainly pace,
Her folds of skin that work and row
Beneath the earth-soiled hovel in which she moves.

And so he strains beneath her housey walls
And catches her trouser-legs in his beak
Suddenly, or her skinny limb,
And strange and grimly drags at her
Like a dog,
Only agelessly silent, with a reptile's awful persistency.

Grim, gruesome gallantry, to which he is doomed.
Dragged out of an eternity of silent isolation
And doomed to partiality, partial being,
Ache, and want of being,
Want,
Self-exposure, hard humiliation, need to add himself on to her.

Born to walk alone,
Forerunner,
Now suddenly distracted into this mazy sidetrack,
This awkward, harrowing pursuit,
This grim necessity from within.

Does she know
As she moves eternally slowly away?
Or is he driven against her with a bang, like a bird flying in the dark
        against a window,
All knowledgeless?

The awful concussion,
And the still more awful need to persist, to follow, follow, continue,
Driven, after aeons of pristine, fore-god-like singleness and oneness,
At the end of some mysterious, red-hot iron,
Driven away from himself into her tracks,
Forced to crash against her.

Stiff, gallant, irascible, crook-legged reptile,
Little gentleman,
Sorry plight,
We ought to look the other way.

Save that, having come with you so far,
We will go on to the end. J

TORTOISE SHOUT

I thought he was dumb,
I said he was dumb,
Yet I've heard him cry.

First faint scream,
Out of life's unfathomable dawn,
Far off, so far, like a madness, under the horizon's dawning rim,
Far, far off, far scream.

Tortoise *in extremis.*

Why were we crucified into sex?
Why were we not left rounded off, and finished in ourselves,
As we began,
As he certainly began, so perfectly alone?

A far, was-it-audible scream,
Or did it sound on the plasm direct?

Worse than the cry of the new-born,
A scream,
A yell,
A shout,
A pæan,
A death-agony,
A birth-cry,
A submission,
All tiny, tiny, far away, reptile under the first dawn.

War-cry, triumph, acute-delight, death-scream reptilian,
Why was the veil torn?
The silken shriek of the soul's torn membrane?
The male soul's membrane
Torn with a shriek half music, half horror.

Crucifixion.
Male tortoise, cleaving behind the hovel-wall of that dense female,
Mounted and tense, spread-eagle, out-reaching out of the shell
In tortoise-nakedness,
Long neck, and long vulnerable limbs extruded, spread-eagle over her
house-roof,
And the deep, secret, all-penetrating tail curved beneath her walls,
Reaching and gripping tense, more reaching anguish in uttermost
tension
Till suddenly, in the spasm of coition, tupping like a jerking leap, and
oh!
Opening its clenched face from his outstretched neck
And giving that fragile yell, that scream,
Super-audible,
From his pink, cleft, old-man's mouth,
Giving up the ghost,
Or screaming in Pentecost, receiving the ghost.

His scream, and his moment's subsidence,
The moment of eternal silence,
Yet unreleased, and after the moment, the sudden, startling jerk of
coition, and at once
The inexpressible faint yell—
And so on, till the last plasm of my body was melted back
To the primeval rudiments of life, and the secret.

So he tups, and screams
Time after time that frail, torn scream
After each jerk, the longish interval,
The tortoise eternity,
Agelong, reptilian persistence,
Heart-throb, slow heart-throb, persistent for the next spasm.

I remember, when I was a boy,
I heard the scream of a frog, which was caught with his foot in the
mouth of an up-starting snake;
I remember when I first heard bull-frogs break into sound in the spring;
I remember hearing a wild goose out of the throat of night
Cry loudly, beyond the lake of waters;
I remember the first time, out of a bush in the darkness, a nightingale's
piercing cries and gurgles startled the depths of my soul;
I remember the scream of a rabbit as I went through a wood at
midnight;
I remember the heifer in her heat, blorting and blorting through the
hours, persistent and irrepressible;
I remember my first terror hearing the howl of weird, amorous cats;
I remember the scream of a terrified, injured horse, the sheet-lightning

And running away from the sound of a woman in labor, something like
      an owl whooing,
And listening inwardly to the first bleat of a lamb,
The first wail of an infant,
And my mother singing to herself,
And the first tenor singing of the passionate throat of a young collier,
      who has long since drunk himself to death,
The first elements of foreign speech
On wild dark lips.

And more than all these,
And less than all these,
This last,
Strange, faint coition yell
Of the male tortoise at extremity,
Tiny from under the very edge of the farthest far-off horizon of life.

The cross,
The wheel on which our silence first is broken,
Sex, which breaks up our integrity, our single inviolability, our deep
      silence
Tearing a cry from us.

Sex, which breaks us into voice, sets us calling across the deeps,
      calling, calling for the complement,
Singing, and calling, and singing again, being answered, having found.

Torn, to become whole again, after long seeking for what is lost,
The same cry from the tortoise as from Christ, the Osiris-cry of
      abandonment,
That which is whole, torn asunder,
That which is in part, finding its whole again throughout the universe.

THE END

www.ingramcontent.com/pod-product-compliance
Lightning Source LLC
LaVergne TN
LVHW091252080426
835510LV00007B/228